The Reformation
in Germany
and Switzerland

Pamela Johnston
Head of History,
St Swithun's School, Winchester
and
Bob Scribner
Fellow of Clare College,
Cambridge

CAMBRIDGE
UNIVERSITY PRESS

PUBLISHED BY THE PRESS SYNDICATE OF THE UNIVERSITY OF CAMBRIDGE
The Pitt Building, Trumpington Street, Cambridge, United Kingdom

CAMBRIDGE UNIVERSITY PRESS
The Edinburgh Building, Cambridge CB2 2RU, UK   http://www.cup.cam.ac.uk
40 West 20th Street, New York, NY 10011–4211, USA   http://www.cup.org
10 Stamford Road, Oakleigh, Melbourne 3166, Australia

First published 1993
Second printing 1999

Printed in the United Kingdom at the University Press, Cambridge

A catalogue record for this book is available from the British Library

ISBN 0 521 40607 2

Maps by Jeff Edwards

Cover illustration Portrait of Martin Luther (1483-1546) 1529 (oil in panel)
by Lucas Cranach, the Elder (1472-1553)
Galleria degli Uffizi, Florence/Bridgeman Art Library, London/New York

GO

Contents

Acknowledgements

Pamela Johnston would like to thank her colleagues and students at St Swithun's School Winchester for helpful comments and suggestions, and Rosemary Duke in particular. Initial work was conducted while Pamela Johnston was Schoolteacher Fellow at New Hall, Cambridge; the collaboration of the two authors emerged from discussions on this occasion. Thanks are due to Rosemary Duke and John Morrill for suggesting the possibility of collaboration, and to Stephanie Boyd and John Morrill for constructive criticism, advice and encouragement. The book was written while Bob Scribner was British Academy Marc Fitch Research Reader at Cambridge University. He expresses his gratitude for the time free from teaching and administrative duties.

The authors and publishers are grateful to the following for permission to reproduce illustrations and extracts:

Documents 8.8 J. Calvin, *Institutes of the Christian Religion*, ed. J. T. McNeill, Library of Christian Classics, SCM Press, London, 1960; 1.1, 1.2, 1.5, 1.11, 6.13, 6.14 H. J. Hillerbrand, *The Reformation in its Own Words*, SCM Press, London, 1964; 1.7 *Luther's Works. American Edition*, Fortress Press, Philadelphia, 1957; 6.4, 6.5 P. Matheson (ed.), *The Collected Works of Thomas Müntzer*, T. & T. Clark, Edinburgh, 1988; 6.7 *Mennonite Quarterly Review*; 1.9(a) J. C. Olin (ed.), *Desiderius Erasmus. Selected Writings*, Harper & Row, New York, 1965; 4.1–4.5, 4.7, 4.8, 4.10, 4.11, 5.11(a), 6.8 T. Scott & B. Scribner, *The German Peasants' War. A History in Documents*, Humanities Press, Atlantic Highlands, 1990; 8.12(b) *Two Treatises of Servetus on the Trinity*, Harvard University Press, Cambridge, Mass., 1932; 1.6, 1.8 B. L. Woolf (ed.), *The Reformation Writings of Martin Luther*, Lutterworth Press, London, 1953.

Figures 1, 2 British Museum, Print Room; 6 Schweizerisches Nationalmuseum, Zurich; 3 The Warburg Institute; 5, 12 Staatsbibliothek Berlin, Handschriften Abteilung; 7 The Scolar Press; 8, 9 British Library,

London; 10, 11 Dietz Verlag, Berlin; 13 Germanisches Nationalmuseum, Nuremberg; Map 1 Hamish Hamilton, London; Map 2 Edward Arnold, London.

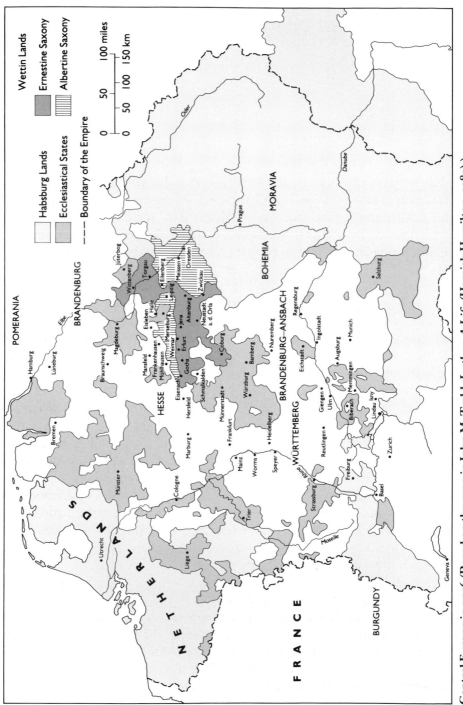

Pomerania

Brandenburg

Hamburg
Luneburg
Bremen
Braunschweig

Magdeburg
Juterbog
Wittenberg
Torgau

Mansfeld
Eisleben
Halle
Eilenberg
Meissen
Dresden

Munster
Frankenhausen
Muhlhausen
Merseburg
Leipzig
Zwickau

Cologne
Hersfeld
Eisenach
Gotha
Weimar
Erfurt
Jena
Altenburg
Neustadt a. d. Orla

Hesse
Marburg
Schmalkalden
Coburg

Liège
Frankfurt
Munnerstadt
Bamberg
Würzburg

Utrecht
Heidelberg

N E T H E R L A N D S

Brandenburg-Ansbach

Nuremberg
Regensburg

Mainz
Worms
Speyer

Trier

Eichstadt
Ingolstadt
Augsburg
Munich

Württemberg

Giengen
Ulm
Memmingen

Strassburg
Reutlingen
Lindau
Isny
Biberach

Freiburg
Basel
Zurich

F R A N C E

Burgundy

Geneva

Bohemia

Prague

Moravia

Salzburg

Elbe
Oder
Danube
Rhine
Moselle

Wettin Lands

Ernestine Saxony

Albertine Saxony

Habsburg Lands

Ecclesiastical States

— — — Boundary of the Empire

0   50   100 miles
0   50 100 150 km

Central Europe in 1546 (Based on the map in John M. Todd, *Luther. A Life* (Hamish Hamilton, 1982).)

Introduction

The purpose of this book is to bring together documents that reflect some
recent approaches to the Reformation in Germany and Switzerland. Older
histories of the Reformation overemphasised the towering figure of Luther
and focused almost exclusively on his theology. Much of the complexity of
the Reformation was lost thereby: popular reactions to Luther, which often
did not follow his ideas in ways he would have found acceptable; the
manner in which ideas of religious reform became embroiled with
demands for social and political reform; the variety of ways in which a
reform of religion was understood. The fact that reform began in
Switzerland under the influence of Zwingli, more or less independently of
Luther, has too often been downplayed. The social aspects of religious
reform, especially where they involved political dissent or rebellion, were
also presented as though they had little to do with Reformation ideas. The
religious radicals, usually associated with Anabaptism, were presented as
unimportant and marginal figures. The difficulties of setting up a new
church and institutionalising reform received no attention at all. No
recognition was given to the fact that the Reformation took a long time to
establish itself among the German population at large, that it was very
much a 'long, slow Reformation'. Consequently, the significance of
Calvinism was not always clear, namely, that it represented an attempt to
establish a more thorough type of reform, arising from an awareness that
the first generation had been less than successful and had made too many
compromises with the old religious system.

The documents that follow, many of them appearing in English for the
first time, attempt to correct these misemphases. They focus on the
heartlands of the Reformation in Germany and Switzerland and cover its
first half-century, roughly 1515–64. Documents have been chosen to show
the interaction of religious reform with the political, social and economic
concerns of all levels of society, rulers and ruled, urban and rural.
However, a special emphasis has been given to popular aspects of reform,
providing a view of the different ways ordinary people responded to the

ideas of Luther and others. The documents also attempt to give full weight to the social issues which developed alongside the theological problems of the day, and to bring Zwingli, Calvin and more radical figures fully into the story. They reveal the many difficulties of turning theological ideas into religious practice, not least because of basic disagreements among the reformers themselves. The implementation of religious change was also a political matter, and the documents show many different aspects of the Reformation's political progress below the level at which the story is often told, namely, the high politics of the Empire. The politics of the Reformation most often involved the politics of local communities, especially the problems encountered in spreading new ideas to a predominantly peasant population.

The documents do not attempt to provide a complete narrative of the main events of the Reformation in Germany and Switzerland. There are many excellent treatments of these events which readers may consult (see 'Suggestions for further reading'). This introduction also dispenses with such an outline, since the introductory sections to each chapter and for individual documents provide all the necessary background information. Read as a whole, these sections constitute an ongoing narrative of the main developments of the Reformation in which the documents are located. Here it will suffice to signpost the issues addressed in each chapter. The story begins with the 'Luther affair' and the manner in which it developed from an academic debate among churchmen and intellectuals into a public and political scandal of international dimensions. Support for Luther and attacks on him stirred up a hornet's nest of controversy, fuelled by the involvement of humanists and carried by the propaganda media of the popular pamphlet, the broadsheet and the ballad. Under pressure of controversy, Luther elaborated on his initial ideas to produce increasingly radical statements which drew the religious issues into a whirlpool of social and political debate. Thus, Chapter 1 concentrates on how Luther became a public figure and the myths that quickly surrounded him to make him an object of popular adulation. Chapter 2 deals with the ferment and turbulence caused by the first practical changes that flowed from Luther's ideas, especially the restructuring of church life in Wittenberg. It also examines more negative consequences such as popular anticlericalism, and how people in town and country began to form their own ideas about religious reform, especially about the contribution of the 'Word of God' to the improvement of social and communal life. The political implications of introducing radical changes in the organisation of religion are also reflected in documents in this chapter. Chapter 3 concentrates on Zwingli and the reform he initiated in Zurich independently of Luther. Zwinglianism was to have a powerful influence in south Germany, not least in propagating a view of religious reform more orientated to social issues and to popular action. Such tendencies came to a head in the German Peasants' War, the focus of Chapter 4. Here rural and urban rebels adapted central ideas of the Reformation, such as the Bible and the Word of God as the ultimate standard of judgement in Christian life, to demand redress of socio-economic grievances and to envisage a restructuring of society and government on evangelical lines. The German Peasants' War also marked a watershed in Luther's attitudes towards the popular aspects of reform. In effect, Luther turned his back on 'reform from below' and supported a controlled 'reform from above', in the hands of secular rulers and especially the princes.

Chapter 5 deals with two issues on which deep-rooted forms of popular belief presented considerable barriers to thoroughgoing religious reform. Debates on the role of images in religious belief and on how Christ was said to be present in the bread and wine of the Eucharist grew into two major controversies that provoked bitter disagreement among the reformers and split the emergent Reformation into divergent tendencies. The theme of diversity is taken up again in Chapter 6, where religious radicals such as the Anabaptists, for many years overlooked or marginalised in the story of the Reformation, are allowed a voice. The documents here reveal the broad spectrum of religious radical thought, as well as some of the distinctive ways it was put into practice. Chapter 7 concentrates on attempts over the following decades to consolidate the religious changes introduced in the 1520s. It reveals the difficulty of institutionalising reform by government action, especially of communicating the fervour of religious leaders to the population at large, above all to countryfolk. It poses the question of how far the Reformation might be said to have been successful at the level of the average rural parish. The final chapter deals with 'the second generation' of reform initiated by Calvin in Geneva, a reform marked by dissatisfaction with the efforts of the first generation. Calvin's approach to reform demanded clearer definition of belief, greater moral rigour and stricter discipline in the propagation of religious renewal. Calvin provided the inspiration for the second great wave of reformation during the second half of the sixteenth century and into the seventeenth, although such developments necessarily lie outside the scope of this book.

It only remains to comment on how these documents are intended to be used. Historians use documents in many complex ways. As well as analysing the contents of a document for what it says and does not say, they also compare one document with another, pursuing themes progressively revealed across several documents. They take account of the author's background and the particular interests he or she had in producing the document. They also seek to uncover ideas, attitudes and approaches which an author did not consciously intend to reveal and which are often only of secondary importance to the main purpose of the document – for example, the frequent references Luther makes to the activity of the devil in the events of the Reformation. Readers should try to make use of the documents here in all these ways, guided by the questions suggested for consideration throughout, and by the 'Themes for comparative investigation' provided at the end. However, these are only intended as rough guidelines. Documents are most exciting to use when readers set out on their own voyage of exploration, discovering in them views and interpretations not singled out by the editors.

1 The Luther affair

The German Reformation began with Luther and the controversy over indulgences in which he became embroiled from 1517. The ensuing debate was at first confined to the world of learning: theologians, scholars and humanists. However, it quickly became a matter of concern to a wider public, involving the question of Roman dominance of the German church, the 'tyranny' of church law and the nature of papal authority. It developed political as well as theological ramifications, catapulting Luther into the public eye as a figure of controversy. As he became better known to a broader public, his 'cause' was taken up by many folk who at first had little understanding of the principles and insights that moved him to his initial protest. Humanists saw in him a fellow spirit in their struggle against scholastic narrowness and in their attacks on the monastic orders. Firebrands such as Ulrich von Hutten saw Luther as an ally in his own campaigns against overbearing prelates and for the revival of German cultural values, analogous to the revival of Italian culture in the wake of the Renaissance. Political authorities became aware of the potential for social unrest implicit in Luther's ideas, and regarded him as a threat to order, even where they were sympathetic to his attacks on Rome. The commons in town and countryside reacted differently, seeing Luther as a holy man who spoke the truth about deception and revealed to them the light of the Gospel. Some saw him as a prophet sent from God, almost a living saint. It was the last image of Luther that was to be taken up and disseminated by propagandists for 'Luther's cause', making him in his own day so much a figure of legend and mythology that it is almost impossible to discern the real man beneath the myth. However, it was this popular response that turned the 'Luther affair' into a far-reaching upheaval in church and society.

1.1 Tetzel's preaching of indulgences: Friedrich Myconius's account

Friedrich Myconius, the Reformer of Gotha, wrote in the 1530s the first brief history of the beginning of the Reformation in Saxony. His version of the nature of Tetzel's preaching, written from his own reminiscence of it, became the standard account of the origins of the 'Luther affair'.

At that time a Dominican monk named Johann Tetzel was the great mouthpiece, commissioner and preacher of indulgences in Germany. His preaching raised enormous sums of money which were sent to Rome. This was particularly the case in the mining town of Annaberg, where I, Friedrich Myconius, listened to him for over two years. The claims of this shameful monk were unbelievable. Thus he said   5 that if some had slept with Christ's dear mother, the pope had power . . . to forgive as long as money was put into the indulgence coffer . . . He furthermore said that if they would put money quickly into the coffer, all the mountains near Annaberg would turn into pure silver. He claimed that in the very moment the coin rang in the coffer, the soul rose up to heaven. In sum, and substance: God was no longer   10 God, as he had bestowed all divine power on the pope.

H.J. Hillerbrand, *The Reformation in its Own Words*, London, 1964, p. 44

1.2   Luther's protest against Tetzel's activity

Luther heard reports of Tetzel's preaching from subjects of the Elector of Saxony who went to buy indulgences from him. His outrage at what he heard about popular reactions to the indulgences led him to write a letter of protest to Archbishop Albert of Mainz on 31 October 1517, the date traditionally assumed by Lutheran historians as the beginning of 'the Reformation'.

There is sold in the country under the protection of your illustrious name the papal indulgence for the building of St Peter's in Rome. In this I do not complain so much about the great clamour of the indulgence sellers, whom I have not personally heard. But I am greatly concerned about the false notion existing among the common people which has become a cause of public boast. These unfortunate   5 souls seemingly believe they are assured of their salvation as soon as they purchase letters of indulgence. They also believe the souls leave purgatory as soon as they put the money in the chest . . . The instructions to the indulgence commissioners issued under your name state – surely without your knowledge and consent – that one of the most precious graces offered is the gift of man's reconciliation with   10 God, and the remission of all punishments in purgatory. It is also said that those who purchase such letters of indulgence need not be contrite.

Hillerbrand, *Reformation in its Own Words*, p. 50

Questions

1   To whom is this protest addressed?
2   What was the ostensible aim of selling this papal indulgence?
3   What was an indulgence, and why was it seen as so important by so many people?

4   What outrageous claims were made for indulgences?
5   What underlying conflict would encourage Luther to voice his
    criticisms of Tetzel?
6   Why would Frederick the Wise react favourably to them?

1.3   The Ninety-five Theses

Luther prepared for academic debate at the University of Wittenberg a
series of theses discussing the issues he believed were at stake in the
matter. According to a later legend, these were posted on the university
noticeboard, the doors of the castle church at Wittenberg, but this cannot
be proved. The theses gained wider significance by being published
without Luther's knowledge and consent and circulated to scholars and a
Latin-reading public outside Wittenberg. There were three editions of the
theses published in 1517, reaching at most an audience of a thousand
readers. However, their combative tone, a result of being written for debate
within academic circles, soon made their author more widely known, and
embroiled Luther in a public dispute he had not sought. Only a few of the
theses are given here to show the tone and direction of Luther's argument.

1. When our lord Jesus Christ said 'Repent' . . . he meant that the whole life of
believers should be one of repentance.
6. The pope can remit no guilt, but only declare and confirm that it has been
remitted by God . . .
13–16. The dying will pay all their debts by their death; and they are already   5
dead to canon laws and freed from their jurisdiction. Defective spiritual health in a
dying man must needs bring with it a great fear. This fear and horror is sufficient
in itself to constitute the penalty of purgatory . . . There seems to be the same
difference between hell, purgatory and heaven as between despair, near despair
and assurance.   10
20. The pope, by his plenary remission of 'all' penalties, only refers to those
imposed by himself.
21. Hence the preachers of indulgences are wrong when they say that a person
is absolved from every penalty by the pope's indulgence.
27. There is no divine authority for preaching that the soul flies out of   15
purgatory as soon as the money clinks in the collecting box.
35. It is not Christian teaching to preach that those who buy off souls or
purchase confessional licences have no need to repent of their own sins.
43. Christians should be taught that those who give to the poor or lend to the
needy do a better action than if they purchased pardons.   20
50. Christians should be taught that if the pope knew the exactions of the
preachers of indulgences, he would rather have the basilica of St Peter reduced to
ashes than built with the skin, flesh and bones of his sheep.
79. It is blasphemy to say that the insignia of the cross with the papal arms are
of equal value to the cross on which Christ died.   25

81–2. This wanton preaching of pardons makes it difficult for learned men to guard the respect due to the pope against false accusations or at least from the keen criticisms of the laity. For example: 'Why does the pope not empty purgatory for the sake of holy love?' This would be the most righteous of reasons. Meanwhile he redeems innumerable souls for sordid money in order to build St Peter's, a most trivial reason.   30

90. These are serious questions of conscience for the laity. To suppress them by force alone and not to refute them by argument is to expose the church and the pope to the ridicule of their enemies, and to distress Christian people.

Luther, *Werke. Kritische Gesamtausgabe*, Weimar, 1883–1989 (hereafter abbreviated *WA*), vol. 1, pp. 233–5

Questions

1   Why was the doctrine of purgatory controversial?
2   To which points of the doctrine does Luther draw attention in his Ninety-five Theses?

Hans Holbein the Younger, *True and False Forgiveness*.
The illustration shows in its right-hand scene the pope enthroned in the choir of a church (where one might expect to have found an altar), presiding over the purchases of indulgences and the hearing of confession (after payment of a fee). The left-hand scene presents images of true repentance and forgiveness: a 'public sinner', King David and Manasseh all confess their sins directly to God and receive

3 Why did he believe them to be false and misleading?
4 Why did Luther believe the sale of indulgences brought the church into disrepute?
5 To what is Luther referring in thesis 27?
6 How would you explain thesis 50?

1.4 The Leipzig debate, 1519

An important milestone in the controversy was the Leipzig debate, arranged in an attempt to settle the bitter dispute over doctrinal issues that had grown up between one of Luther's major opponents, Johann Eck, a Dominican friar and professor at the University of Ingolstadt, and Carlstadt, Luther's colleague at the University of Wittenberg, who was to play a leading role in the beginnings of reform. Luther was drawn in at a late stage, focusing his preparatory contribution on the supremacy of the pope. The debate was conducted as a typical academic disputation, each

his forgiveness without intermediary or payment of money. King David was a traditional figure of the repentant sinner, as was Manasseh, who ruled wickedly in Jerusalem for fifty-five years before being punished by God with loss of his kingdom; he repented in prison in Babylon and was forgiven by the Lord (2 Chronicles 33: 10–13). In medieval art, he was depicted as a counterpart to the repentant Mary Magdalene.

side attempting to score points from the other in gladiatorial style. Eck succeeded in trapping Luther into voicing support for the condemned heretic John Hus, to the dismay of the presiding prince, Duke George the Bearded of Saxony, whose lands had suffered devastation from Hussite invasions in the fifteenth century. Duke George was subsequently to become one of Luther's sternest opponents among the German princes.

Luther's report of the debate, 20 July 1519
The following week Eck debated with me, first of all quite sharply concerning papal primacy . . . Then he went to the extreme and emphasised exclusively the Council of Constance, where the articles of Hus asserting that the papacy derived [its authority] from the emperor had been condemned. There he stood quite boldly, as if on a battlefield, and reproached me with the Bohemians and called me   5
publicly a heretic and a supporter of the Hussite heretics. He is an impudent and foolhardy sophist . . . Here I publicly asserted that some articles were condemned at the Council of Constance in a godless manner, since they were taught openly and clearly by Augustine, Paul and even Christ himself.

The third week we debated concerning repentance, purgatory, indulgences and   10
about the power of a priest to absolve . . . Indulgences were thrown out of the window and he agreed almost completely with me. Indeed, the defence of indulgences became plainly a laughing stock, while I had expected it to be the main point of the disputation. In his sermons Eck conceded all this so that even the common people observed his disregard for indulgences. He is even said to have   15
admitted that he would have agreed with me in all points had I not debated about the authority of the pope.
WA Briefwechsel, vol. 1, p. 422

Questions

1   How did the Leipzig debate change the nature of the controversy?
2   Why did the supremacy of the pope become an issue?
3   What was the significance of associating Luther with Hus?
4   Why does Luther call Eck 'an impudent and foolhardy sophist'?

1.5   Luther's reluctance for public controversy

Luther always stated that he had no intention of causing turmoil in the church, but was forced by bitter attacks on him to defend his own position. In the course of doing so, he began to develop more radical ideas which gradually alienated him from the official church. In 1520 he wrote an open letter to Pope Leo X, defending the stance he had taken. There is no reason to believe that he was not serious in expressing his puzzlement about how the affair developed.

It is a mystery to me how my theses . . . were spread to so many places. They were
meant exclusively for our academic circle here. This is shown by the fact that they
were written in a language that the common people could hardly understand. They
were propositions for debate, not dogmatic definitions, and they use academic
categories. Had I anticipated their widespread popularity, I would certainly have   5
done my share to make them more understandable. What shall I do now? I cannot
recall my theses and yet their popularity makes me hated. Unwillingly I must enter
the limelight and subject myself to the dangerously shifting judgement of men. I
am no great scholar. I have a stupid mind and little education – this in our
flourishing century whose superb literature would even push Cicero into a   10
corner . . . Necessity forces me to be a honking goose among singing swans.

Hillerbrand, *Reformation in its Own Words*, pp. 50, 54

Questions

1 Why does Luther deprecate his own learning, considering he was a
   professor of theology?
2 How much of this extract is written for rhetorical effect?
3 How would you decide whether Luther's tone is sincere?
4 What do you think he hoped to achieve by it?

1.6 Luther's position becomes more radical

Whatever his initial intentions, Luther's response to his opponents' attacks
was to think through more completely the implications of his own
theological positions. This led him into radical criticism of the existing
structures of the church, its worship and its sacramental system. The first
public sign was his tract of 1520, *On the Babylonian Captivity of the Church*,
written in Latin, but one which quickly earned him the label of a dangerous
heretic, especially associated with the Hussite heresy.

I confess that the works [of my opponents] benefited me greatly. Although I denied
divine jurisdiction to the papacy, I admitted human jurisdiction. But when I heard
and read the most ingenious arguments put forward by these gentlemen to
establish their idol in a workmanlike manner . . . I saw clearly that the papacy was
to be understood as the kingdom of Babylon.   5
    The first thing for me to do is to deny that there are seven Sacraments and for
the present to propound three: baptism, penance and the Lord's Supper . . .
Elsewhere I have written that the Bohemians had no assured support . . . when
they sought to prove the use of the Sacrament in both kinds [that is, bread and
wine] . . . If, however, in the Lord's Supper either kind could be denied to the   10
laity, so also might a part of the rites of baptism and penitence be withheld from
them . . . The priests must never receive only one kind as Mass, and the reason
given is that two kinds constitute the full and complete Sacrament and should not
be sundered . . . If the church has the authority to withhold the wine from the laity,

she can also withhold the bread; and on the same basis, she could withhold the   15
whole sacrament from the laity, and deprive the laity altogether of what Christ
instituted. But I deny she has that authority . . . I conclude therefore that to deny
both kinds to the laity is impious and oppressive, and it is not in the power of any
angel, nor of any pope or council whatever to deny them . . . Each person should
be allowed a free choice in seeking and using the Sacrament, just as in the case of   20
baptism and penance.

But there is another misconception to be done away with . . . namely, the
common belief that the Mass is a sacrifice offered to God . . . But what we call the
Mass is a promise made by God for the remission of sins . . . Where there is the
Word of a promise-keeping God there is needed the faith of a person who accepts   25
it. It is plain that our salvation begins in our faith . . . From all of which you will see
that nothing else than faith is needed for a worthy observation of the Mass . . . It
follows that the Mass is not a work in which others can share, but an object of
faith . . . and is meant to nourish and strengthen the personal faith of the
individual . . . Now the closer our Mass resembles that first Mass of all, which   30
Christ celebrated at the Last Supper, the more Christian it will be.

There is no scriptural warrant whatever for regarding marriage as a
Sacrament . . . there is no mention of either a divine institution or a promise which
together would constitute a Sacrament . . . With regard to the impediments to
marriage, in respect of which the pope claims power to grant dispensations, but   35
which are not mentioned in Scripture . . . all those marriages are valid . . . The
union of man is in accordance with divine law, and this holds good no matter how
it may contradict any regulations made by men . . . In regard to divorce, it is still a
subject for debate whether it should be allowed. For my part I have such a hatred
of divorce that I prefer bigamy to divorce . . . Christ permitted divorce, but only in   40
case of adultery.

Ordination was unknown as a Sacrament to the church of Christ's time . . . It is
the duty of priests to preach and baptise . . . Now we who have been baptised are
all uniformly priests by virtue of that very fact. The only addition received by the
priests is the office of preaching, and even this with our consent . . . Those whom   45
we call priests are really ministers of the Word and chosen by us; they fulfil their
entire office in our name. The priesthood is simply the ministry of the Word . . .
The function of the priest is to preach; if he does not preach, he is no more a priest
than the picture of a man is a man.

**The Reformation Writings of Martin Luther, edited by B.L. Woolf,
London, 1953, pp. 208–309 *passim***

Questions

1   Why were Luther's ideas on the Sacraments such a threat to the
    church?
2   What were the implications for religious practice of Luther's ideas on
    each of the Sacraments he mentions above?

3 Explain the significance of identifying the papacy with the kingdom of Babylon?

1.7 Luther on Christian liberty

Luther's most explosive ideas were contained in a tract written in German, *On the Liberty of the Christian*. This encapsulated his characteristic doctrine of justification by faith, but also drew wide-ranging consequences for Christian behaviour. It was this doctrine that gained the widest appeal and which provoked the widest controversy as to how far the common people had understood it or not.

I shall set down the following two propositions concerning the freedom and the bondage of the spirit: A Christian is a perfectly free lord of all, subject to none. A Christian is a perfectly dutiful servant of all, subject to all . . . One thing and only one thing is necessary for Christian life, righteousness and freedom. That one thing is the most holy Word of God, the Gospel of Christ . . . The Word of God 5 cannot be received and cherished by any works whatever, but only by faith. Therefore it is clear that, as the soul needs only the Word of God for its life and righteousness, so it is justified by faith alone and not by any works . . . Thus, the believing soul by means of the pledge of its faith is free in Christ, free from all sins, secure against death and hell, and is endowed with eternal righteousness . . . Yes, 10 since faith alone suffices for salvation, I need nothing except faith exercising the power and domination of its own liberty. This is the inestimable power and liberty of Christians.

   Not only are we the freest of kings, we are also priests forever . . . for as priests we are worthy to appear before God to pray for others and to teach one another 15 divine things . . . You will ask, 'If all who are in the church are priests, how do those whom we now call priests differ from laypeople . . .' [They are only those] who should according to the ministry of the Word serve others and teach them the faith of Christ and the freedom of believers. Although we are all equally priests, we cannot all publicly minister and teach. 20

Luther's Works. American Edition, Philadelphia, 1957, vol. 31, pp. 344–6, 355–6 *passim*

Questions

1 What does Luther understand by 'Christian freedom'?
2 What are the practical implications of his views?
3 How do you think his ideas could have been interpreted by others so that they 'misunderstood' them?
4 What is Luther suggesting about the nature of priesthood? Why might this appear particularly threatening to the clergy?

1.8   Luther's appeal to the ruling elites of the Empire

Although Luther's ideas about Christian liberty struck a popular chord, he did not wish to provoke popular unrest or upheaval. In a third tract of 1520, he appealed to the Christian nobility of the Empire to intervene to reform religion, the church and many social abuses, advancing 'twenty-seven proposals for improving the state of Christendom'. His ideas on social reform were not new, and merely echoed long-standing German calls for reform. Moreover, his attacks on the Roman and papal church found a ready response among ruling elites long hostile to foreign influence in Germany. The real radicalism resided in the dismantling of an entire legal, political and institutional framework implicit in his reform ideas.

Every prince, noble and city should strictly forbid their subjects to pay annates to Rome . . . No secular matter is to be referred to Rome . . . The far-reaching and fearful oaths which bishops are wrongfully compelled to swear to the pope should be abolished . . . Since this example of oppression hinders the bishop from exercising his proper authority . . . then an obligation falls on the emperor and the   5
ruling classes supporting him to repel and punish it as a piece of tyranny. The pope should exercise no authority over the emperor . . . The pope should withdraw from temporal affairs . . . Pilgrimages to Rome should be disallowed . . . No more mendicant houses should be built . . . Would to God they were all dissolved or all combined into two or three Orders . . . These Orders must also abandon   10
preaching, unless they are called upon to do so by the bishops, pastors, churches or civil authorities.

We know also how the priesthood has declined. Many a poor priest is responsible for wife and child . . . Each single town should have a pastor or bishop . . . and that pastor shall not be compelled to live without a wife . . . As the   15
Apostle Paul teaches us plainly, the method to be followed among Christians is that each town should choose from its church a scholarly and devout citizen, and lay upon him the duties of a pastor; his maintenance being cared for by the church. He should be quite free to marry or not.

Masses on anniversaries or at celebrations and for the dead ought to be entirely   20
abolished or at least reduced in number . . . Excommunication must never be employed as a penalty, except where the Scripture prescribes its use, that is, against those who believe amiss or who live in open sin . . . All feast days should be abolished . . . The degrees within which marriage is forbidden should be altered . . . The question of fasting ought to be a matter of free choice . . . The   25
extra-parochial chapels and churches should be pulled down. I mean those which have recently become the goal of pilgrimages . . . The saints should be allowed to canonise themselves . . . Probably one of our greatest needs is to abolish all begging everywhere in Christendom . . . Confraternities, indulgences . . . ought to be drowned and destroyed as containing nothing good . . . It is high time we took   30
up the Hussite question and dealt with it seriously . . . The universities need a sound and thorough reformation.

We shall now devote a section to the consideration of temporal failings . . .
There is urgent need of a general order . . . against the overflowing abundance and
great expensiveness of the clothing worn by so many nobles and rich folk . . . We   35
do not need to waste such huge sums for . . . imports from abroad . . . In the same
way the spice traffic ought to be reduced . . . But the greatest misfortune suffered
by the German people is the traffic in annuities . . . We must surely bridle the
Fuggers and other similar trading companies . . . The next thing is the abuse of
eating and drinking . . . Finally, is it not a lamentable thing that we Christians   40
should openly tolerate in our midst public brothels, though we all took an oath of
chastity at our baptism?

Reformation Writings of Martin Luther, vol. 1, pp. 109–200 *passim*

Questions

1 List the reforms suggested by Luther in 1.8. What do these reveal of
   his own prejudices as well as his genuine passion for change?
2 Discuss the implications of Luther's recommendations for reform.
3 How would they have changed social and political life in Germany?
4 Why did Luther appeal to the 'Christian nobility' to carry out reforms?
5 What is meant by the terms 'mendicant houses [**line 9**],
   'confraternities' [**line 29**], 'annuities' [**line 38**]?
6 Who were the Fuggers and why did Luther suggest that they should be
   restrained?

1.9   Humanist reactions to Luther
1.9(a)   *Erasmus' Axioms on behalf of Martin Luther, Theologian*

Erasmus was very circumspect in his public statements about the 'Luther
affair'. However, in November 1520 he drew up a series of twenty-two
statements for the guidance of Frederick the Wise, from which a selection
is offered here. Because they were not intended for publication and
Erasmus was worried lest they fall into the wrong hands, they probably
represent his true feelings about the 'Luther affair'.

The origin of the case is evil: the hatred of letters and the desire for supremacy.
The way in which it is being conducted corresponds to its origin, with wild cries,
plots, bitter hatred, poisonous writing. Those who are conducting the case are
open to suspicion. Since all the best and closest to Gospel teaching are said to be
the least offended by Luther. It is well known that certain men take advantage of   5
the good nature of the pope. All the more should their rash advice on this case be
shunned. The case is tending toward a greater crisis than certain men suppose.
The severity of the bull [condemning Luther] offends all upright men as unworthy
of the most gentle vicar of Christ. It should be considered all the more diligently by

persons who are above suspicion and who are experienced in these matters. Only   10
two universities . . . have condemned Luther, and they have . . . not convicted him
of error, nor are they in agreement . . . Luther is not soliciting anything; therefore
he is less suspect. The interest of others is being pressed. For the pope the glory of
Christ comes before his own, and what is of profit to souls takes precedence over
any other advantage . . . Difficult matters press upon us and the guidance of [the   15
emperor] Charles should not be defiled by such hateful measures. It seems to the
advantage of the pope that this affair be settled by the mature deliberation of
serious and impartial men; in this way regard will best be shown for the dignity of
the pope. Those who up to now have written against Luther are disapproved of
even by theologians who otherwise are opposed to him. The world thirsts for   20
Gospel truth, and it seems to be carried in this direction by a longing ordained, as
it were, by fate. Therefore, opposition to Luther ought to be without hate.

**Desiderius Erasmus. Selected Writings, edited and translated by John C.
Olin, New York, 1965, pp. 147–9**

1.9(b)   *Ulrich von Hutten's political response*

The firebrand imperial knight and humanist, Ulrich von Hutten, found in
Luther's ideas confirmation of his hatred of the clergy and of foreign
influence. He was inspired to call upon fellow Germans to repudiate
Roman trickery and to wage an anti-clerical war, publishing several
polemical tracts and dialogues on the theme. Hutten's strident tone and
call to the 'German nation' to rouse itself in Luther's support led to him
being depicted alongside Luther as a champion of 'German liberties' (see
p. 25).

*Complaint and Admonition Against the Overweening Unchristian Power of the Pope at
Rome and the Impious Clergy.*

The die is cast. This I have dared.

I want to complain, if I may,
And everyone the truth to say,
To make the general errors clear
And of many crimes you must hear   5
Through which the nation is aggrieved
And all the German lands deceived.
All morals now are quite upturned,
All godly doctrine is but spurned,
In blindness to the Christian truth   10
Where false belief now rules the roost . . .

He who for the truth will stand
With bans is hounded from the land
This is not godly and not right
He who against it will not fight   15
Will be with God in dire disgrace
I warn him of his evil case . . .

I hope there will soon awake
All Germans bold, who then will stake
Their lives in this as I have done   20
In protest, though I stand alone.
I call upon the nobles proud
And pious towns all in a crowd
To join me in the common cause
For which I fight without a pause.   25
Take pity on your fatherland.
O worthy Germans, raise your hand
The time is here, the fight begun
For freedom, which through God is won . . .

Arise, you pious Germans, come!   30
For armoured horse in goodly sum,
Halberd, pike and sharpened sword
Stand ready, and where warning word
Will not help, then we must fight.
Stay not to ask if this is right.   35
Do not stay to ask for leave
God's aid and vengeance cannot deceive

We punish only godless men,
Arise and let's go to it then,
For in our cause we act aright   40
And have good reason that we fight.
God's Word they have turned upside-down
The Christian folk with lies confound'd
Let us wipe the lies away
And the light of truth upon them play   45

Arise, we have the grace of God!
Stay not at home, but come along
Thus have I dared – this is is my song.

E. Böcking, *Ulrich von Huttens Schriften*, Leipzig, 1859–70, vol. 3, pp. 475–6, 525–6

Questions

1   Compare the reactions of Erasmus and Hutten to the 'Luther affair'.
2   To whom did they appeal to support Luther?
3   What different action would have been taken in the 'Luther affair' if their advice had been followed?
4   How important was Hutten's role in rallying support for Luther?

1.10   Luther at the Diet of Worms
1.10(a)   *Report of the Venetian ambassador*

April 25: I cannot tell you how much favour Luther enjoys here. It is of such a nature that I fear it will produce some bad effect after the emperor departs and the diet breaks up, especially against the prelates of Germany. In truth, had this man been prudent and restricted himself to his first propositions and not entangled himself in manifest errors about the faith, he would have been not just favoured,   5
but adored by the whole of Germany.

1.10(b)   *Papal Legate Aleander reports from Worms*

To Cardinal Medici, February 1521
A little while ago in Augsburg they were selling Luther's picture with a halo [see p.25]; it was offered without a halo for sale here, and all the copies were gone in a thrice before I could get one. Yesterday I saw on one and the same page Luther depicted with a book and Hutten with a sword. Over them was printed in fair   5
letters: 'To the fair champions of Christian Liberty, M. Luther and U. von Hutten' [see p.25]. The world is so far gone that the Germans press around these two scoundrels in blind adulation, and adore even during their lifetime the men bold enough to cause a schism . . . And I am given up to such people!

P. Kalkoff, *Die Depeschen des Nuntius Aleander vom Wormser Reichstag*, Berlin, 1898, pp. 34, 52

Questions

1   Compare the two viewpoints expressed in **1.10(a)** and **1.10(b)**.
2   What does the Venetian ambassador mean by 'his first propositions' [**1.10(a), line 4**]?
3   How far were the ambassador's views borne out by future events?
4   What was the effect of linking Luther and Hutten in the depiction cited by Aleander?
5   What was the effect of depicting Luther with a halo?
6   How was Aleander trying to protect his own position?

Luther as Saint.
Luther is here depicted as a friar, identified by his large tonsure and his friar's frock and cowl, holding the open book of the Bible. The halo identifies him as a living saint.

Luther and Hutten as Champions of Christian Liberty.
The Latin captions attest the humanist origins of this double depiction.

1.11   A reconstruction of Luther's speech before the diet

Most serene lord Emperor, most illustrious princes, most gracious lords . . . I ask
you to observe that my books are not all of the same kind. There are some in which
I have dealt with piety in faith and morals with such simplicity and so agreeably
with the Gospels that my adversaries themselves are compelled to admit them to
be useful, harmless and clearly worth reading by a Christian. Even the bull, harsh   5
and cruel as it is, makes some of my books harmless, though it also condemns
them . . . The second kind consists in those writings levelled against the papacy, as
against those who by their wicked doctrines and precedents have laid waste
Christendom by doing harm to the souls and bodies of men. No one can either
deny or conceal this for universal experience and grievances are witness to the fact   10
that through the pope's laws and man-made teachings the faithful have been most
pitifully ensnared, troubled and racked in torment, and also their goods and
possessions have been devoured, especially among this famous German nation, by
unbelievable tyranny . . . If I recant these, it will only add strength to such
tyranny . . . The third kind of those books I have written against private   15
individuals . . . I confess I have been more harsh against them than befits my
religious vows and profession. For I do not make myself out to be any kind of saint,
nor am I contending about my conduct, but about Christian doctrine. But it is not
in my power to recant them.

    Your imperial Majesty demands a simple answer. Here it is plain and   20
unvarnished. Unless I am convicted of error by the testimony of Scripture, by
manifest reasoning I stand convicted by the Scriptures, and my conscience is taken
captive by God's Word. I cannot and will not recant anything, for to act against our
conscience is neither safe nor open to us. On this I take my stand . . . I can do no
other. God help me. Amen.   25

Hillerbrand, *Reformation in its Own Words*, pp. 89, 91

Questions

1 Summarise the main points of Luther's speech.
2 Explain the reference to the bull. What did it say about Luther's
   writings?
3 Which of Luther's writings gave most offence? Did he stand by all of
   them for the same reasons and with the same conviction?
4 What does he mean by 'tyranny' [line 14]?
5 Was Luther's answer as 'plain and unvarnished' [lines 20–1] as he
   claimed?
6 What was the significance of Luther's appeal to 'the testimony of
   Scripture' [line 21]?

1.12 Luther enters mythology: *Dr Martin Luther's Passion*

This popular pamphlet reveals the kind of adulation and propaganda that began to surround Luther in the highly charged atmosphere following the Diet of Worms. The full weight of the parody will be appreciated if you read St John's Gospel, chapter 18, from verse 28.

Luther and disciples went forth over the river Rhine and entered into Worms, where Caesar was holding a diet. Knowing that he had come, the high priests and pharisees assembled into the palace of the high priest of Mainz, called Caiaphas, and consulted with the scribes how they might betray his safe-conduct, and take him by subtlety and burn him. But they said: not during the diet, lest there be an 5 uproar among the people. Then while Luther was in the house of Knights of St John, Carraciolo called Pedico and Aleander the Jew sought to betray him with the kiss of peace. But Luther, knowing all things that should come upon him, went forth and said unto them: 'Whom seek ye?' They answered him: 'Dr Luther.' Luther said unto them: 'I am he.' 10

When morning was come the high priests and the papists took counsel against Luther, that they might burn him with fire. Then they took him and turned him over to the archbishop of Trier, and he inquired of him: 'Art thou a doctor of the gospel and the truth?' And Luther said: 'Sayest thou this thing of thyself or did the Romanists tell thee of me?' And the archbishop said: 'Am I a Romanist? They who 15 cannot endure the Gospel truth and the words of Paul have delivered thee to me. What hast thou done?' Luther answered as a Christian: 'My writings do not concern this world but God . . .' And Trier asked: 'Art thou a doctor of evangelical truth and of St Paul?' And Luther answered: 'Thou hast said it. To this I was born, and for this I came into the world, that I should restore to their pristine purity the 20 words of the Gospel and of St Paul, because the papists have distorted them to their own use and for the Roman Curia, to the great detriment of the German nation.'

Then the governor saw that it did no good and that a great tumult was made among the people, that is among the Romanists because they displayed much 25 money and great dignities. Having then taken water and washed his hands in the presence of the people, he said: 'I am innocent of the blood of this Christian man, as you see.' And all the clergy and the Romanists answered: 'His blood be upon our heads.'

Then the governor delivered to them the books of Luther to be burned. The 30 priests took them, and when the princes and people had left the diet they made a great pyre in front of the high priest's palace, where they burned the books; and they placed on the top a picture of Luther with the inscription: 'This is Martin Luther, the doctor of the Gospel'.

Doctor Mar. Luthers Passio, durch Marcellum beschrieben, Augsburg, **1521**

Questions

1 When the writer refers to the 'high priest of Mainz' [**line 3**] and 'the governor' [**line 24**], whom does he have in mind?
2 Who were the Romanists [**line 25**]? What is the significance of comparing them to the Jews in St John's Gospel?
3 How close is the narrative to events at the Diet of Worms?
4 Which sentence provides a good summary of Luther's aims and opinions?
5 Which groups of people would have most appreciated the parody?
6 Comment on the significance of comparing Luther with Christ.

1.13   Propaganda for Luther's cause

1.13(a)   *Complaint of a layman, Hans Schwalb, over the many abuses of the Christian life, 1521*

Some priests say that when a man is under the ban he should be cut off from the Christian church, and cannot merit good works. As one well knows, a person was recently drummed out of the church of St Severus and placed under the ban because he had accompanied the pious Martin Luther, who speaks the truth without fear of men. How can anyone be so damnable that he would outlaw any   5
man or eject him from the Christian community, and heed the ban more than the words of Christ. Does it not say in the Gospel (Matthew 7:1) 'judge not lest you be judged'? Is that not damnable, to order a man out of the church or otherwise ban him?

The worthy Dr Martin speaks the truth as Christ and the apostles spoke it, but   10
each of our priests contradicts this truth and says: 'Whoever believes the words of Dr Martin does not believe aright and is against God.' And when they hear that some villagers have taken a mind to believe Dr Martin's words, they dare to say that they will not bless their village bells. Thus, one shuts the mouths of wicked villagers by forbidding them the Sacraments, as it is said confirmation has been   15
refused recently. Is that godly or right? Or have you read somewhere that you may do this to such pious wicked folk? I'll warrant you that you have learned that from your diabolical lord the pope, who also wanted to withhold the Christian Sacrament. When the Greeks wanted to convert to the Christian faith and join us, the pope thought he could become rich, and set them a great sum of money to pay   20
each year in perpetuity. The poor folk would not do that; they thought that Christ had allowed his faith to be proclaimed free . . . But our priests increase the faith of Christ the way the wolf does the sheep. That's why there are so many fat sheep.

O. Clemen, *Flugschriften aus den ersten Jahren der Reformation*, Leipzig, 1907–11, vol. 1, pp. 348, 355

1.13(b) *The spiritual wolves*

A woodcut broadsheet, probably published in 1520 or 1521, depicted Luther's opposition to the spiritual wolves who prey on the flock of Christ. Note the division of the woodcut into two areas of darkness and light.

The text reads:

Look at this strange beast, a wolf clad in churchly dress, rampaging among the sheep; a red hat runs after it, there is the wolf's cousin. Beware, you sheep, run not away from him who hangs on the cross. Let this wolf run his course, he will sell a kingdom in hell. He has eaten many a sheep, and is to be accounted as equal to Satan. The shepherds have become wolves. They are not content to shear the sheep. The flock that they should shepherd is scattered, strangled by false doctrine. This greatly saddens my heart, as I see the great harm visited upon Christendom by pope, cardinal and bishop. Ezeckiel has prophesied of this. Thus I preach and teach and write, even at the cost of my life.

1.14 A personal view of Luther, August 1523

It has been difficult for historians to disentangle Luther from either the hostility of his opponents or the adulation and mythmaking of his supporters. The Polish diplomat and humanist, Johannes Dantiscus, was curious to see what kind of person the famous reformer was, and when returning home from an embassy to Spain in 1523 he made a detour via Wittenberg. His view of Luther, written immediately afterwards to the bishop of Posen, Johann Latalski, is noteworthy as that of someone uninvolved in the polemical debates of the early Reformation. It perhaps brings us closer to Luther's personality than any other contemporary account.

Perhaps from excessive curiosity, I did not want to pass up the chance to see Luther, who was then not far away in Wittenberg. However I could not get there without some difficulty. The rivers, especially the Elbe, which flows through Wittenberg, were so swollen that all the grain in the river flats was flooded. On the way there I heard many words of abuse and curses against Luther and his cronies   5
because of this flood. For there is a general belief that God has afflicted the land because they have eaten meat during the forty days of Lent.

I found there several young men who were extraordinarily learned in Hebrew, Greek and Latin, especially Philip Melanchthon, who claims the leading position among them because of his knowledge and learning. He is a young man of 26 and   10
was very genial and obliging to me during the three days I spent there. Through him I explained the purpose of my journey to Luther in the following terms: whoever had been in Rome and not seen the pope, or in Wittenberg and not seen Luther would be thought by common opinion not to have seen anything . . . I went with Melanchthon to see him after a dinner, to which he had invited some friars of   15
his order. These were recognisable as friars, since they wore white habits, although in the manner of soldiers, but in their hair style there was nothing to distinguish them from farmers [i.e. they wore no tonsure].

Luther stood up and offered me his hand – he was rather touched, it seems – and bade me be seated. We sat down and discussed various matters and issues for   20
four hours, well into the night. I found the man witty, learned, eloquent, except that he had little to say of the pope, the emperor and other princes other than abuse, arrogant imputations and snappishness. If I were to write it all down it would take more than a day, and the messenger who is to take this letter is ready to depart, so I must summarise much in little. Luther's features are like the books he   25
publishes: the eyes are sharp and have a strange sparkle, as the eyes of obsessives are wont to do . . . His speech is vehement, full of mockery and taunts. He wears clothes which are indistinguishable from those of a courtier. But when he returns to where he lives (the former Augustinian monastery), so I have been told, he puts on his friar's habit.   30

When we were sitting with him, we did not just engage in discussion, but merrily drank wine and beer, as is the custom there. He seemed to me to be, as the Germans say, 'a merry fellow'. Now as far as the holiness of his life is concerned, about which there is much talk among us, he did not seem any different from any one of us. One can immediately recognise in him haughtiness and great desire for   35
fame; in abuse, mockery and scorn he seems almost frolicsome. How he is in other manners one can see from his books. He is said to be very well read and to write a

great deal. At the moment he is translating the books of Moses from Hebrew into Latin, in which he frequently requires Melanchthon's help. This young man pleases me by far the best of all the scholars of Germany, and also does not agree   40 with Luther in everything.

Inge Müller-Blessing, 'Johannes Dantiscus von Hofen. Ein Diplomat und Bischof zwischen Humanismus und Reformation', *Zeitschrift für die Geschichte und Altertumskunde Ermlands* **31/32 (1967/8), pp. 149–50**

Questions

1   What insight is gained from **1.14** regarding
    (a) Luther's personality
    (b) unfavourable opinions of Luther?
2   Comment on the sentences beginning
    (a) 'Whoever had been in Rome . . .' [**line 13**]
    (b) 'Now as far as the holiness of his life is concerned . . .' [**line 33**]
3   Can you relate the comments about Melanchthon to the role he subsequently played in the Reformation?
4   What further comments would you make about the usefulness and significance of this document?

2 The rise of the reform movements

It did not take long before those supporting 'Luther's cause' turned to more direct action in his support. The continuous discussion, teaching and preaching of Luther's supporters in Wittenberg that had been going on throughout the years 1517–20 began in 1521 to lead to liturgical changes, especially in the Mass. Ardent supporters such as Gabriel Zwilling and Andreas Bodenstein von Carlstadt wanted radical reform at once. They led by example and were followed by many students, impatient for change in matters such as worship, the use of images and clerical marriage. This first wave of reform was regulated by the town council, before the town's ruler, the Elector of Saxony, stepped in to prohibit it and to enforce a slower and more conservative pace of change, but even in the initial stages, the secular ruler intervened out of concern for social unrest.

2.1 Chancellor Gregor Brück to Elector Frederick the Wise, 11 October 1521

This letter was written in answer to a query from the Elector of 10 October 1521.

It is said that Master Gabriel Zwilling, the preacher in the Augustinians, has preached the following: first, that the most worthy Sacrament of the altar should not be adored, for it was not so instituted according to Christ's intentions but was meant purely in his memory. It is idolatry and superstition where it is so used that it is adored. Second, the Mass cannot be celebrated, as has previously happened, 5 without sinning, rather all who attend Mass should partake of the Sacrament and receive it under both species [of bread and wine]. Third, it follows that the monks and others should not be forced to hold [private] Mass, as they have been forced to do by their prior, for in this way the Sacrament, which is for the purpose of communion, is not properly used. 10

N. Müller, *Die Wittenberg Bewegung 1521 und 1522*, Leipzig, 1911, pp. 188–90 (no. 10)

2.2 A university committee reports to Frederick the Wise, 20 October 1521

At the Elector's request, a university committee was set up to investigate the unprecedented events in Wittenberg. Its report served to explain and to justify them. Almost all members of this committee subsequently played leading roles in the further development of the Reformation, among them Philip Melanchthon, Andreas Bodenstein von Carlstadt, Justus Jonas and Nikolaus von Amsdorf.

Gracious lord, at your request we have investigated the Augustinians and found that they have ceased to hold Mass for three reasons . . . First, because a great and unchristian abuse of the Mass has been implanted throughout the whole world, both spiritual and secular . . . Second, the celebration of the Mass as it has hitherto been observed is contrary to the usage and practice instituted by Christ and the   5
Apostles . . . Third, Christ commanded and instituted that both specics be given [to the laity].
   It is certain that the abuse of the Mass is one of the greatest sins on earth . . . and there is no doubt that we will be severely punished with wars and plagues . . . For the Mass is in its most prominent part no more than a spiritual meal . . . and   10
this spiritual meal is no more than a sure sign, when a lay person goes to the Sacrament, by means of which we are reminded of the forgiveness of sins . . . From which it follows that the Mass is no good work at all, through which one might offer or give anything to God.

Müller, *Wittenberg Bewegung*, pp. 195–200 (no. 16)

Questions

1 Who were the Augustinians?
2 Why might Chancellor Bruck's report in 2.1 have caused concern to the Elector of Saxony?
3 How did the university committee explain and justify events in Wittenberg?
4 Notice that both 2.1 and 2.2 focus on change in the meaning and practice of the Mass. Why do you think this was so? Do the demands made here follow on from Luther's teaching? (2.1 and 2.2 will be useful for comparison when studying Chapter 5.)
5 How did such events follow on from Luther's teachings?
6 Where was Luther at this time?
7 Why did events develop so radically in his absence?

2.3   A news report from Wittenberg (shortly after 6 January 1522)

Matters developed quickly in Wittenberg over the autumn and winter, until more violent forms of direct action were being taken as a result of following the logic of the new theological views. This anonymous report was probably written by Ambrosius Wilcken, a parson from the nearby village of Dobien.

[An account of] what has happened since St Barbara's Day (4 December). Since then only one Mass has been held each day . . . and all the other Masses have ceased. In the Franciscan cloister, the students approached the friars and almost tore down a wooden altar and they stuck a threatening letter on the church door, so that the friars went in fear and had to post guards . . . Some of the Franciscans   5
preach more strongly against the Mass than anyone else . . . and admonished the people not to go to hear such Masses, if they cared about the salvation of their souls.

Doctor Carlstadt has not celebrated Mass for some time now, but since he preached most abominably at the one Mass he did celebrate, the canons decided   10
that in future no one would deputise for him when he had to celebrate a feast; to which he said that if he had to celebrate Mass on his next feast day, New Year's Day, then he would hold an evangelical Mass, as Christ had instituted.

The requiems, commemorations, thirty-day commemorations and anniversaries have all been abolished. On 26 December Doctor Carlstadt, accompanied by two   15
wagonloads of bold and learned folk such as the Provost Justus Jonas and Philip Melanchthon, betrothed himself to marry a young maiden, the child of a poor nobleman. At the same time the parson promised himself in marriage to his own cook and married her shortly thereafter.

Doctor Martin was secretly in Wittenberg for three days this past Advent,   20
dressed like a nobleman in a frockcoat, and he has grown a thick beard over his lips and cheeks such that his closest friends did not recognise him at first.

The commune of Wittenberg presented the town council with articles which they undertook to uphold and for which they would commit their life and goods . . . The town council wrote to the Elector about the articles, but he   25
requested that they be suspended until he could issue a mandate. But the community would not be satisfied with this in the mid-term, so that on New Year's Day communion was administered in both forms, with the bread and the chalice, to several thousand. There were just as many who communicated with the body and blood of Christ on the following Sunday (5 January) and on the feast of the   30
Epiphany (6 January).

Item, Carlstadt preached twice each Friday. I believe that the entire town was present, [including] all those who rarely if ever went to the sermon, for now no one would miss it. Some also began to render a Psalm into German and to expound it on each workday . . . And Carlstadt reads a passage from the Bible that the priests   35
do not like to hear . . . The princes will not be able subdue it or repress it, try as they will; but if it comes from God, we will see miracles. In all the little towns around about many strange tales are told. May God grant us his grace. Amen.

Müller, *Wittenberg Bewegung*, pp. 406–9 (no. 68)

2.4   Hermann Mühlpfort, student in Wittenberg, to Hermann Mühlpfort, mayor of Zwickau, 1521

It is not known whether or in what way the student Hermann was related to his namesake in Zwickau. Luther dedicated his tract on Christian liberty to the Zwickau mayor with good reason, for Zwickau was one of the earliest Saxon towns after Wittenberg formally to introduce religious reform.

There is such dissension and disagreement here, not only among the citizens but also among some of the scholars, both secular and clerical . . . It so happened that a friar in the Augustinian cloister [Zwilling] preached very sternly against the Mass, saying that it should no longer be celebrated, and said publicly that all those who hear or attend the Mass commit sin . . . This has caused such confusion   5
among the community that they do not know where they are.

Now it happened that on the following Monday [2 December] two priests came to the city church and wanted to read Mass. As they came to the altar some citizens and students rushed forward and forcibly took the mass-books from the altar, threw the candles and candlesticks around the church so violently that they   10
bounced, and drove the priests from the church so that they could not say Mass. The same happened on the Tuesday and Wednesday [3 and 4 December] . . . A public notice was posted on the Franciscan church threatening that if the Mass was not stopped, this would be done with force and its celebration forbidden. Then on the Friday night [6 December] around forty noblemen and students   15
marched around with pipe and drum until midnight, all of them well armed. They had the intention that evening of storming the monastery and striking dead any monks they could lay hands on. The town council intervened to prevent this. Meat was eaten the whole week through . . . and the students wanted to display their Christian freedom by this means.   20

Ernst Fabian, 'Zwei gleichzeitige Berichte von Zwickauern über die Wittenberger Unruhen 1521 und 1522', *Mitteilungen des Altertumvereins für Zwickau und Umgegend*, 11 (1914), pp. 26–8

2.5   Latest news from Wittenberg, from Johann Pfaban to Hermann Mühlpfort, mayor of Zwickau, 1522

Daily there is preaching against the entire estate that we have hitherto called 'the spiritual estate' and regarded as holy, and that the Masses that have hitherto been celebrated by the priests are almost all diabolical, and everywhere evangelical Masses have been celebrated. But everywhere there is no agreement about the matter, so some do not confess beforehand to a priest but only to God and   5
celebrate Mass in faith. Some think that to confess to another layperson, to accuse oneself and to receive absolution is an important matter. Some say that confession is unnecessary. Still, the canon is commonly omitted from the Mass by all priests, the people are given communion under both kinds, the priests and monks allow their tonsures to grow out and take wives.   10

Moreover, and more horrible to hear, Master Gabriel [Zwilling], who put off his cowl here in Wittenberg, left the Augustinian order and put on secular dress. On

Friday [10 January] he made a fire in the courtyard of the Augustinian monastery, went into the church with them and completely broke up the wooden retable altar, and carried this and other panels, painted and carved images, crucifixes, banners,   15 candles, church lights, etc. to the fire, threw them in and had them burned. He helped to cut off the heads of stone images of Christ, Mary and other figures and helped to strip all paintings from the church. On the following Sunday [12 January] he preached, indicating the cause of his actions and of the burning, and presented the people with the bread of the Sacrament, saying to everyone who   20 desired it that they should take it into his or her own hands and receive it. Afterwards he travelled from Wittenberg to Eilenberg, where he administered the Sacrament in the same way, and preached so strongly against the clergy that the common folk there stormed the parsonage . . . and some folk were arrested because of it.   25

Fabian, 'Zwei gleichzeitige Berichte', pp. 28–30

Questions

1   What further changes do **2.3–2.5** show taking place in late 1521?
2   What is meant by 'evangelical Masses' [**2.5, lines 3–4**]?
3   What is revealed in **2.3** about the way Wittenberg was governed?
4   Why did Luther return in disguise?
5   What does **2.3** tell us about
    (a) changes in the behaviour of the clergy
    (b) changes in the way services were conducted
    (c) the effects of these events on Wittenberg as a whole?
6   What was the impact of these events and what was the response to them, as shown in **2.4** and **2.5**?
7   What evidence of violence is found in **2.4** and **2.5**? Who were the perpetrators and what were their aims?
8   Why is no account taken of this violence in **2.3**?
9   What later became of Zwilling?

2.6   Gothard Schmalz, The 'Parson Storm' in Erfurt, 1521

Meanwhile, in places outside Wittenberg, support for religious reform quickly became involved with wider issues. This sometimes took the form of violent anticlerical outbursts, as occurred in Erfurt on 11–12 June 1521. A student riot was provoked by charges of heresy levelled at those who supported Luther when he passed through Erfurt on his way to Worms. The Erfurt town council was not slow to exploit this incident to their own advantage, forcing the city's clergy to sign an agreement on 29 July 1521, ceding clerical privileges. Such events were typical of the rapid spread of the reform movements in the towns, posing problems of social order and legality for urban authorities. The author of this account was possibly a student, and may have been an eyewitness to the riot.

Now listen, good friends, I hear that there is a rumour going around that some days ago in the town of Erfurt the clergy and students had some business with each other. I think Dr Martin had been in Erfurt, and his theme was 'Peace be with you' . . . When he came to the town many of the clergy took it ill, but those who received him also had the tonsure.   5

It began with Kessel, whose house on the Horsemarket was stormed. He cried 'Murder!' and 'To arms! Oh, awful fright, my door is broken down!' And if he had not run away, he would have been in for a fight. The righteous parson of St Vitus lived not far away and they stove in his door, so that he almost shit himself in his bed, so great was his fear. The others cried out 'Strike boldly!', and they set   10 Wiedemann to rights. They threw his servant in the river and punched him in the head. Oh, how the poor wretch blubbered! . . . I too was in the first hubbub . . . They smashed up all his chambers, kicked and chucked all his pots and pans about, and threw them about the house so that nothing escaped damage. They poured beer on all his books . . . and guzzled down all his Rhenish wine –   15 Wiedemann had already fled. Otherwise they took nothing besides the cash lying around in the room.

On they went, and all ran up the hill to 'The Green Door' . . . [and] 'The White Wheel' also took its turn [these were both houses in which the church court sat] . . . Who did not get a good blow in there? 'Strike freely, you'll find knavery   20 enough here to vex many a man . . . Many a false oath was taken there . . . Here many a maid had to take a man against her will.'

Thereafter they came to Kirchmer's house, but he got rid of them with fair words. But another band came up later and said to him: 'Have you not done more [than you pretend]? The plague upon him! He has often written to [the archbishop   25 of] Mainz with the secrets of the town council, and brought harm to Erfurt.'

They came to the Reverend Peter Muss's house on the corner, and wanted to give him a good fright . . . for he is a great liar, and when he stands in the pulpit lets no true word leave his mouth . . . The third band came, so I hear, to Rottendorfer's house. One said to another: 'He brought a whore from Würzburg,   30 has been a canon here for fourteen years and not said a single Mass . . . Set boldly to!' . . . 'They broke down his door . . . but Hermann, his best servant, said: 'Listen, good fellows, my lord is a good Martinist, by God, and here stands beer, bread and wine for you.' They entered the room . . . and one swept the food boldly from the tables, bowls and glasses, great and small . . . They smote in the windows   35 until they rang, tore up letters and books, smashed tables, ovens and stools, and the symphony went on until nothing remained standing in the kitchen . . . Thus one should treat whoring priests!

Clemen, *Flugschriften*, vol. 1, pp. 361–73.

2.7   Treaty of the Erfurt town council with the clergy, 29 July 1521

This treaty was typical of many agreements forced upon the clergy in the
wake of the turbulence precipitated by the reform movements.

1 We [the clergy] will reveal to the worthy council whatever goods we have both
inside and outside Erfurt, and in other places. We will submit such goods to
taxation, and pay one per cent wealth tax and the assessment, the same as other
citizens.

2 We will allow secular properties we have acquired from citizens to be returned 5
to them whenever they so request, for the price we paid for them . . .

3 We will take no more than four per cent interest on all annuities in the town
and the council's territories, and all bonds will be attested with the council's
seal . . .

4 We will acquire no secular properties from citizens or subjects of the council 10
by purchase, brokerage or in other ways, without the permission of the council.

5 We will wholly refrain from malting and brewing.

7 We will not sell, serve or exchange our wine in secret, so that the council loses
its excise.

8 We should and will refrain from all citizen trade, such as in wool, hay, corn, 15
hops, cloth, shearing cloth, innkeeping, buying and selling, or making loans
thereto, nor form any companies with citizens or outsiders for this purpose.

9 We will pay the excise on slaughtering as completely as the citizens, and will
not import meat secretly.

10 We will likewise pay the milling excise. 20

11 We will not evade the poll-tax on our servants.

12 We will burden no citizen or subject of the council with spiritual demands
[i.e. citations before church courts], but will have such persons [with whom we
have disputes] called before the town bailiff or the rural officials, where we will
receive speedy redress. 25

Stadtarchiv Erfurt 0–1/I 55

Questions

1   How reliable does the account in **2.6** seem to be?
2   What were the motives which impelled the students to stir up a riot
    against the clergy of the cathedral chapter?
3   What can be deduced from the style of the passage about the popular
    reaction to these events?
4   (a) What does **2.7** reveal about clerical privileges?
    (b) How had these privileges been abused?
5   Detail the ways in which **2.6** and **2.7** explain the strength of anticlerical
    feeling in Erfurt.

2.8   A Dominican disputes with a journeyman baker in Augsburg, 1523

Evangelical fervour quickly created problems of order in German towns, as zealous adherents of the new ideas sought to uphold their viewpoint against the orthodox clergy, leading to numerous confrontations of the kind described below. The example shows the new-found confidence of lay Christians and the consequences of evangelical preaching for female piety.

On St Margaret's Day, 13 July 1523, a Dominican preached at St Margaret's convent about how pregnant women should pray to St Margaret, for St Margaret had begged God that when pregnant women invoked her, they should be given relief, and God had promised her this. Now as the monk was about to lead the public confession of sin, a journeyman baker called Joerg Fischer spoke up and   5
begged to interrupt the friar in the pulpit, saying: 'Good sir, you have preached about St Margaret', and asking where that was found in Scripture. The friar replied: 'Where the devil cannot come, he sends his messenger.' The baker retorted that he should not preach such things, for he misled the people. Whereupon the friar said that he would report him to the authorities. Then the   10
baker said that if he could prove in Scripture what he had preached was the truth, he was willing to suffer whatever penalty had to be endured. Whereupon the friar had a fainting fit, sinking down and saying: 'Oh, Mary, Mother of God, what is happening to me!' and asked the nuns to come to his aid, for he was weak. Several women complained about the baker, but some women took the baker's side. Then   15
a nun screamed out loudly, telling the baker that the citizens had allowed Dr Urbanus [Rhegius, the evangelical preacher] and him to dine in their houses and they had made love to their wives. Whereupon an old woman said to the nun that she was a liar, 'and you would gladly have someone make love to you, but no one wants you!' The journeyman baker went to the town council to report on the   20
events, and some thought that he should be punished, but the matter was let drop.

Chroniken der deutschen Städte, vol. 25, Leipzig, 1896, p. 199

Questions

1   What had happened to make the baker more aware of Scripture?
2   What does **2.8** suggest about the changing role of laypeople?
3   What effect did this new outlook have on the popular attitude to saints?
4   How does this link to **2.4** and **2.5**?

2.9   Four citizens of Giengen an der Brenz petition the town council for an evangelical preacher

An important stage in the development of the evangelical movement in any urban community was to petition the town council for the appointment of an evangelical preacher. This posed considerable difficulty if the town council was conservative and there was no widespread popular pressure for reform, as was the case in the tiny imperial city of Giengen. The arguments advanced, however, are wholly representative of the 'urban Reformation'.

[The town council provides for food and fuel for those in need, so why does it not meet the needs of those who have great hunger of the soul, which cannot be satisfied except with the Word of God?] Faith comes from hearing, hearing from a sermon, a sermon from a preacher. Now if the preacher presents his audience with pure wheat without any chaff, then his table companions will eat the finest white   5
bread; if it is digested, it will form clear, refined and natural blood, good blood gives a good constitution, a good constitution constant health, good health gives good work and good work brings honour and praise. Now the Word of God is the fine white bread presented by the preachers; the table companions are the people who hear the Word of God; if they accept diligently they will digest it; if they digest   10
it with reflection on the why and wherefore, it will bring pure blood, and so they will learn to understand what God is, what proper honour of God is, what is a right faith, what proper good works are, what man is and how man can do nothing good unless a continually healthy conscience makes him constant in all temptations, so that he rests on God and his divine Word as on a rock. Such a sound and constant   15
conscience brings form and moderation to all deeds and action. From this springs the good works that are pleasing to God.

Thus it is our humble desire and plea to the worthy Council, in God's name, for an upright, honourable, virtuous, godfearing Christian preacher . . . Now if the worthy Council thinks it good and useful, we would like to have the Rev. Hans the   20
curate, for this reason: he has hitherto presented the Word of God faithfully to the whole community. And if the worthy Council sees financial difficulties thereby, we would beg the worthy Council to retain him for a while at our expense . . . But if the worthy Council will not approve this, we will desist from our request as continually obedient and willing subjects . . . The worthy Council should not heed   25
the fact, as some folk say, that he [Hans] is an unknown and despised person and no Doctor or Master of Theology . . . for Holy Scripture is sealed to all the wise, powerful and learned of this world who have never understood and will not understand it until the end of the world . . . so it does not matter a hair whether he is a Doctor of Theology or not, or even a bishop, a pope or a sowherd or some   30
other despised person.

S. Andler, 'Die Reformation in Giengen a.d. Brenz', *Blätter für württembergische Kirchengeschichte*, 1 (1897), pp. 98–100

Questions

1   How do the petitioners draw out their parable of preaching and fine white bread?
2   What are the qualifications of the Reverend Hans?
3   How do the petitioners anticipate objections?
4   How do they defend themselves against accusations of rebellion?

2.10   Lazarus Spengler, city secretary of Nuremberg, memorandum on religion, 3 March 1525

Civic authorities became increasingly concerned at the impact of religious controversy on social order. Evangelical supporters advanced the argument that it was denial of the Word of God that created disorder and that social harmony could be restored by true preaching of the Word and by prohibiting the activities of the orthodox clergy. This memorandum written for the town council in Nuremberg was the prelude to open adoption of evangelical reforms in Nuremberg by prohibiting Catholic preaching. However, it also reveals that the new ideas had not swept all before them and there was still a very substantial number of Nuremberg residents who adhered to the old religion, indeed who had been won back from their initial attraction to the new ideas.

In this Christian matter touching the Word of God there are two points of utmost grievance that concern Nuremberg alone, about which I as a Christian am also highly aggrieved.

The first is the divisive preaching of the opposing proclaimers of the Word of God . . . I have seen publicly that a great number of Christians in this town are not   5
turned away from their old errors . . . but that the preachers . . . who do not present the Word of God with a clear and right Christian understanding confirm them in their old human ways. Some people who were inclined to the Word of God through Christian preaching, have been misled again by secret and public sermons and by the hearing of confessions as practised hitherto, and their   10
consciences disturbed . . . Second, from such divisive preaching there must certainly follow disunity of magistrates, the dissipation of morale, morals and manners, the fracturing of civic unity and finally disturbance and recalcitrance towards the clergy . . . or against the authorities who look on and permit them [to preach].   15

G. Pfeiffer, *Quellen zur Nürnberger Reformationsgeschichte*, Nuremberg, 1968, pp. 211–12.

Questions

1   Who was Lazarus Spengler, and why was his opinion important?
2   What does he mean by 'divisive preaching' [**line 11**]?
3   What did he believe the result of 'divisive preaching' [**line 11**] to be?
4   What conclusion did he invite his readers to draw?

2.11   The 'Communal Reformation' in the countryside: the demand for godly preachers

Evangelical ideas quickly spread beyond the towns into the countryside. The most powerful form taken by the movement was the demand for godly preachers, elected and paid for by the local community. Blaufelden was a village north of Schwäbisch Hall, in the territory of the margrave of Brandenburg-Ansbach, who decided at a territorial diet in October 1524 that 'the Word of God should be preached purely and clearly according to the Old and New Testament'. The patronage of the benefices was in the hands of the Provost of Neumünster, to whom the margrave would have to apply for a change of incumbent. However, the community phrased their request for a preacher of their choosing as though the margrave had the right to make the change himself.

Grievances of the county of Blaufelden, 1525
We have a parish priest and two other priests in our village, who are of no use to the community, but are harmful, scandalous and ruinous to the salvation of souls, and who display no honourable Christian life or conduct. The parish priest is infirm, and cannot speak well enough to be understood, and he is so infected with   5
bad breath or some odour that he is repulsive to pregnant women or the sick who wish to take the Sacrament . . . Moreover, he cannot preach the holy and divine Word to us, and if he could, we could not hear or understand him. From all that we have been able to hear from him, everything is concentrated on confession fees, hearing Mass, making offerings, founding anniversary masses, holding requiems,   10
paying for sin with such good works, and helping the poor souls of the dead out of purgatory. To sum up, he stinks of greed.
    The second priest, Endress Barttelmess, does nothing among us other than . . . to pursue such financial wheeling and dealing that he has acquired a remarkable amount of wealth here, which could not have been done without considerable   15
harm to the community. The third, Caspar Thull, is much the same . . . Both priests [Barttelmess and Thull] live in open scandal and sin with their mistresses and children, to the great scandal of the entire community and parishioners. What we can see and learn by such Christian behaviour, and what its fruits may be, your princely grace may judge yourself.   20
    We have here a preacher, the Rev. Hans Schilling, whose parents and ancestors grew up among us, and who preaches at our request. We can hear his sermons and he has instructed us diligently from holy Scripture and taught us the holy Christian faith, love of neighbour, and that we should be subject and obedient to our authorities. Although the enemies of the divine Word among us have reported to   25
your princely grace that he preaches seditiously, we beg your grace to dismiss the above-mentioned parish priest and confer the parish on the Rev. Hans Schilling, so that we might be spiritually nourished by the divine Word. But hitherto your princely grace has burdened us with these three priests, whom we must retain, while Hans Schilling has been forbidden to preach by the district official . . . We   30

most humbly beg your princely grace to take this to heart and to think of the salvation of our souls.

G. Bossert, 'Die Reformation in Blaufelden', *Blätter für württembergische Kirchengeschichte,* **6 (1902), pp. 33–4**

Questions

1   Summarise the reasons for the community's dislike of their priests. Why was their attitude towards Hans Schilling different?
2   What stood in the way of appointing Hans Schilling as a preacher?
3   What does **2.11** tell us about the practical application of the community's right to choose its own pastor?

2.12   The politics of reform

It was not always a simple matter to introduce reform, even where a town or prince possessed some kind of sovereignty over a local community. The legal complications created by having to take account of patronage and other rights sometimes tied the hands of the most willing authorities, even those of an imperial city, as the village of Herzogenaurach found in 1524.

The city of Nuremberg to Herzogenaurach, 15 December 1524
[In reply to your letter] concerning your parish priest, who takes ill care of you . . . in communicating the right and true Word of God . . . It falls within the competence of the bishop to act against negligent pastors or benefice holders. Thus, it is not in our power to remove your parish priest from his position. There   5
is also no vacant benefice for which we have the patronage and to which we might transfer your pastor. If he were minded to resign voluntarily or the parish became vacant in other ways . . . then we would know how to behave in a proper Christian manner . . . But if your pastor wants to remain, a virtuous Christian preacher may be appointed alongside him, or if you are unable to agree this with your parish   10
priest, it would not be a bad idea to maintain an evangelical preacher for a time at your own expense, considering how highly you value the Word of God, through which alone we will be saved.

Pfeiffer, p. 313

Questions

1   Why were the authorities in Nuremberg unable to meet the request of the village of Herzogenaurach?
2   Discuss the motives behind the reasons given.
3   What is suggested by the tone of this letter?
4   What do **2.11** and **2.12** show about the political limitations on religious reform?

2.13   The politics of reform: memorandum on the appointment of a preacher in Speyer, 1538

Not all imperial cities were as willing as Nuremberg to advance the evangelical cause by open adoption of religious reform, as shown by Speyer. The new ideas had been preached in Speyer since Luther's appearance at the Imperial Diet in 1521, but the town council was reluctant for various reasons to adopt reform openly. It quickly realised the value of the new doctrines in the long-standing struggle over clerical privilege, and used the confusion of the Peasants' War to subject the clergy to civic obligations. However, the bishop of Speyer, backed by the influence of the Elector Palatine, forced the restoration of all clerical privileges in 1526. The town council was nervous about the possibility of disturbance caused by evangelical preaching, for it feared that the new preachers could be as truculent as the old. It was no less afraid of the political influence and ambitions of the bishop of Speyer and thus unwilling to alienate the emperor. The town also hoped for economic advantage by having the Imperial Court of Chancery located in their town, as it was from 1527.

It has been revealed from the divine Word that man requires that same divine Word for the sustenance of the soul and its salvation no less than the mortal body requires natural bread. Yet it has been noted in the city of Speyer that the divine Word has been little taught . . . and the common folk therefore desire the pure divine Word. However, it is inappropriate that the town council should undertake   5
to appoint or accept a special preacher for the following reasons: first, according to law, such preacherships should not be set up other than with proper permission, in this case that of the bishop. And if this were attempted, it would surely follow that the town council's power to appoint and dismiss him would quickly be removed, whatever he preached . . . and after much trouble and expense, one would be stuck 10
in the same hole as before.

   Second, if the town council appointed a preacher itself without the permission of the bishop, then there would certainly be no other consequence than that it would fall under the deepest suspicion of forgetting everything said by his Imperial Majesty and of adhering to the Lutherans. And with this it would show a particular 15
defiance of his Imperial Majesty . . . which might lead to the final ruin of our city. Besides the new preachers are as little to be trusted as the old priests, for it has been seen publicly that the majority of them seek their own self-interest as much as the old, rather than that of the poor dearly redeemed sheep of Christ . . . And their supporters have learned more stubbornness and innovations from them than 20
they knew or used before. Besides, they have interfered in the secular law even more than the old clergy of the papal gang ever did . . . And however humbly they first revealed themselves . . . as soon as they have brought the common herd to their side and become too strong for the authorities, they then cannot be paid enough, and all brazenness and frivolity . . . is defended and approved with the 25

Word of God. From which much terrible disturbance has arisen in many towns and lands.

Stadtarchiv Speyer I A 450/4

Questions

1   Comment on the date of this document.
2   Why was the Speyer town council so reluctant to allow the appointment of evangelical preachers?
3   Why was the town council disillusioned with the new preaching?

2.14   The problem of the tithe: Nuremberg mandate of 20 May 1524

The preaching of the Gospel opened up many new ideas about social justice, foremost among them the right of the clergy to collect the tithe. In 1523 there were widespread tithe strikes throughout Germany, invoking evangelical ideas in their support. In 1524 this kind of agitation troubled the landed territories of Nuremberg, which moved quickly to prevent the unrest growing into something more sinister by seeking to lay the tithe question to rest. The issue raised questions about the evangelical notion of Christian freedom which were to become of greater importance in the German Peasants' War.

It has come to the attention of the town council of Nuremberg that its subjects . . . in the countryside have undertaken . . . not to pay tithes, rents and interest to their lords . . . To justify their unworthy action, they allegedly defend themselves with the holy Gospel . . . The town council is understandably displeased and aggrieved, and finds that those who undertake this unusual action are unchristian and take up   5 the Gospel in their self-interest and gain, contrary to God's command. True Christians are properly instructed in the Word of God to know that one gives to God what is God's and to secular authority and lordship what belongs to them, and so render to their lords suitable obedience and submissiveness. Moreover, brotherly love obliges each Christian to perform that which he is obliged to do and   10 which he would gladly receive from another. And although each Christian has been freed in conscience through the blood and death of his Saviour, this freedom does not lead to freedom from external burdens.

   Accordingly, it is the worthy town council's request that each and every one of their subjects in the countryside should, because of the obligations by which they   15 are bound, first to the Word of God and then to the worthy council as their secular authority, desist from their unbecoming and unfounded actions, and not ally themselves in word or deed against their authorities, or undertake anything that might infringe their position as subjects. And they should render without hindrance to their lords and others the tithes, rents, interest and dues to which   20 they are obliged by ancient custom.

Pfeiffer, p. 259

Questions

1 What is meant by 'tithes, rents and interest' [**line 2**]?
2 According to this account, what arguments had the rural population given the Nuremberg council against the payment of tithes?
3 List the arguments put forward to refute the people's case.
4 What further threats were made?
5 Why would the council concern itself with these matters?

2.15 Propaganda for reform

The drive for reform was supported and intensified by a wave of printed propaganda, mostly in the form of small pamphlets or single-page illustrated broadsheets. They were meant to be accessible to the unlearned or those with minimal literacy skills, being read aloud and making their message with striking visual images. An example of these broadsheets is provided here. It is a parody of the 'Mass of St Gregory', a depiction of a miraculous vision Pope Gregory the Great experienced while saying Mass which was used to exemplify the doctrine of the Real Presence; this image formed a particular focus for popular devotion to the Eucharist.

Gaze upon this seven-headed beast, quite in the shape and form as St John saw it, a beast from out of the deep, with seven different heads. It was crowned just as this papal beast, signifying the tonsures of the clerical folk. The beast also had ten horns, signifying spiritual jurisdiction and disturbance. It bore a blasphemous name, signifying its seductive tongue. The beast was like a leopard, signifying the   5
murderous kingdom of the pope which executed by tyranny all who opposed him. The beast had feet like a bear's, signifying that the sweet Gospel is trodden underfoot by the papacy and buried, hidden and crushed. The beast has a lion's maw, signifying the papacy's broad hell-mouth, which can never be sated with indulgences, palliums, annates, excommunications, offerings, confessions, mass   10
foundations; it has swallowed everything, rents and interest-payments, peoples, lands and kingdoms. The beast had received a mortal wound, signifying that Doctor Martin has struck the papacy a deadly blow. May God grant that it will soon be overthrown. Amen.

The seven-headed papal beast, Revelation of St John 13, 2 Thessalonians 2

Questions

1 Look up the Bible passages cited in **2.15**, and look at their context.
2 Compare the text of this passage with its illustration.
3 How and why is the papacy compared to a seven-headed beast?
4 Where is the mouth of the beast?
5 What is contained in the locked chest?

6 Why is the cross shown in the background? How can it be identified?
7 What is attached to the front of the cross?

The Seven-headed Papal Beast.

3 Zwingli and reform in Zurich

Religious reform began in Zurich under the influence of Ulrich Zwingli, who became people's preacher (Leutpriester) there at the end of 1518. Although the Luther affair was probably well known in Zurich, Zwingli does not seem to have any direct contact with Luther's works before 1519, and he embarked independently on his own course of reform. The dominant influence on him initially was humanism and local religious and socio-political issues (including the pension system, by which foreign princes such as the king of France or the pope paid pensions to Swiss politicians in order to ensure access to ready supplies of Swiss mercenaries). Influenced by Zwingli's preaching and general activity, Zurich developed between 1519 and 1522 along a wholly different path from Wittenberg, which led to the emergence of a different approach to religious reform, often touching the same issues as those raised in Wittenberg and other parts of Germany, but with characteristic differences.

3.1 Zwingli's evangelical preaching in Zurich, 1519

Zwingli was appointed as pastor on Saturday, 11 December 1518.

Giving thanks for his appointment . . . he said that he had undertaken, with the help of God, to preach on the holy Gospel of St Matthew in its entirety rather than broken up as it was by the prescribed Sunday Gospel readings. He wanted to expound it according to Scripture and not according to human opinions . . . This proposal pleased some in the cathedral chapter, who rejoiced in it, but others believed that such changes and innovations would bring little good. He told the latter than he would not preach innovations but in the traditional way . . . Besides, he would take pains to behave so christianly that no friend of divine and evangelical truth would have just cause for complaint. Whereupon he held his first sermon in Zurich on New Year's Day 1519, the day of his thirty-fourth birthday.   10
    Zwingli's preaching soon gained a following from all kinds of people, especially the common folk. He praised God the Father and taught all persons to trust alone in God's Son, Jesus Christ as their only Saviour. He began to speak out vehemently against false belief, pride and hypocrisy. He spoke firmly of the need for penance, improvement of life, Christian charity and loyalty. He also reproved   15

vices such as idleness, immoderation in eating, drinking and dress, taking pensions
and mercenary service [with foreign rulers] and the repression of the poor. He
insisted most gravely that the magistrates should uphold law and justice, protect
widows and orphans, and that one should endeavour to preserve Swiss freedom
and to reject the lures of princes and lords. The people were divided over this kind 20
of preaching. Some in the community, including the powerful and the clergy,
heard it gladly and praised God for these sermons, but others were less satisfied
and complained greatly about Zwingli, because he could bring great harm to
Zurich.

Heinrich Bullinger, *Reformationsgeschichte*, Frauenfeld, 1838, vol. 1, p. 12

Questions

1   Why was Zwingli such a controversial preacher?
2   What was distinctive about his preaching?
3   What did he attack and what action did he propose?
4   How did people react to his preaching, and why?

3.2   Zwingli combats indulgences, 1519

Zwingli had been preaching vehemently from the beginning of the New Year
against this pardoner [Samson] and his indulgences and dispensations . . . and had
won a considerable following, so that people therefore began to take notice of such
Roman trickery. Around this time (3 March 1519) a general Swiss diet was held at
Zurich. The bishop of Constance had representatives there who were also   5
opposed to Samson, so that when the monk set out from Bremgarten to Zurich . . .
he got only as far as 'The Ox' [an inn on the edge of town], where members of the
Zurich town council warned him that he must not come any further into the city,
for such as he were not wanted there. However as a representative of the pope,
with whom Zurich was still in alliance, he was treated with honour and given some 10
wine.
    The Zurich town council then discussed whether he should be allowed in, and
one witty councillor suggested that he should be allowed in and then taken
prisoner at once and drowned . . . He was allowed to appear [before the Swiss diet
at Zurich], but when people learned what he was about and that he had no direct   15
commission from the pope, he was earnestly told to get out and to leave
Switzerland in a hurry . . . Zwingli also took up the case of this Sanson and dealt
with it very seriously in writing. Envoys who had been sent to Zurich by the bishop
of Constance on his own business were urged by Zwingli – as was Bishop Hugo
himself – to oppose such Roman knavery and deception more boldly than hitherto. 20
The bishop would do real honour to his noble lineage of Landenberg by being one
of the first bishops to uphold and carry forward the Word of God . . . However, the
monk did not stay much longer in Zurich but called it quits and went back to Italy.
After his departure there was much talk of this indulgence in Switzerland, and

about who he had swindled; those of Berne, in particular, mocked him and not   25
long afterwards performed a carnival play about him. And so Zurich was highly
praised for having driven the deceiver away. It also brought much advantage to
Zwingli and to the preaching of the Gospel.

Bullinger, *Reformationsgeschichte*, vol. 1, pp. 14–18

Questions

1 What was Zwingli's reaction to the indulgence-seller Sanson?
2 Why was there such hostility to Sanson?
3 Explain how this incident brought 'much advantage' [**line 27**] to
   Zwingli.
4 How does this incident compare with Luther's challenge to Tetzel in
   1517? Can you suggest why Zwingli was apparently more successful in
   his opposition to indulgences?

3.3   The affair of the sausages, Ash Wednesday, 5 March 1522

Zwingli's preaching against 'human rules and ordinances' which bound the
conscience without bringing improvement was focused by the issue of the
Lenten fast and abstinence, an example of good works which touched
the daily lives of all individuals and which evangelical believers claimed
contributed nothing to salvation. The 'affair of the sausages' was the first
open act of disobedience to the rules of the old church in Zurich.

3.3(a)   *Town council inquiry as to who had been eating flesh and eggs in Lent*

Elsi Flammer, maidservant of the printer [Christoph Froschauer] in Niederdorf,
said that on her master's orders she had cooked some sausages on Ash
Wednesday, and that these were eaten by the people's priest of Einsiedeln (Leo
Jud), by Bartholomew Pur and by Michael Hirt. Afterwards several of her master's
vinedressers had also eaten of this meat.   5
    Bartholomew Pur, the pastrycook, said that on Ash Wednesday he was eating
carnival cakes in the printer's house with Master Ulrich Zwingli, people's priest at
the Great Minster, Master Leo Jud, people's priest at Einsiedeln, Master
Laurence Keller, pastor of Egg, Heinrich Alberi, Michael Hirt the pastrycook,
Conrad Luchsinger and Conrad Escher. The printer produced two dried sausages 10
and they cut them up and each had a piece. All of them ate, except Master Ulrich
Zwingli, people's priest at the Great Minster.

Egli, *Actensammlung zur Geschichte der Zürcher Reformation*, Zurich,
1879, p. 72 (no. 233)

3.3(b)   *The printer, Christoph Froschauer's defence before the council, April 1522*

First, since it has come to your notice that I have eaten meat in my house, I testify as follows: I have so much work to do that it stretches my bodily and material resources. I have to work night and day, workdays and holidays to have things ready for the Frankfurt Fair . . . and I cannot always buy fish. The work is [an edition of] the Epistles of St Paul . . . Second, on reflection I find that almighty and 5 gracious God has blessed and illuminated us with the truth, that is with God's Word, which we must truly believe if we are to be saved, for God has left us nothing on earth in which to trust except the holy Gospel, which is his divine Word, and we must believe this and stand by it; further, that we must direct our lives and actions by the rule of the Gospel, or else we are not Christians.   10

Egli, *Actensammlung*, p. 74 (no. 234)

3.3(c)   *Zwingli on fasting*

To sum up briefly: if you want to fast, do so; if you do not want to eat meat, don't eat it; but allow Christians a free choice. If you are an idle person you should fast often and refrain from food that arouses you; the worker moderates his lusts by hoeing, ploughing and working in the fields. You say: 'But idlers will eat meat without needing to.' The answer is that these very same people fill themselves with 5 luxurious foods, which enflame them even more than salty and spiced meats.

If you would be of Christian temperament, act in this way. If the spirit of your belief teaches you thus, then fast, but allow your neighbour to use Christian freedom. Fear God greatly if you have transgressed his laws, and do not magnify human inventions above what God himself has commanded.   10

Zwingli, *Sämtliche Werke*, vol. 1, pp. 106–7

Questions

1   Sum up in your own words what Zwingli says about fasting. Does it accord with the views of his followers as revealed in 3.3(a) and 3.3(b)?
2   What do 3.3(a)–3.3(c) as a whole reveal about attitudes towards the church and its rules?
3   Was there any positive side to this criticism?

3.4   Zwingli's Sixty-seven Theses, 1523

The religious changes introduced in Zurich under Zwingli's influence led to widespread criticism from the bishop of Constance and other external authorities. The town council therefore decided to stage a public disputa- tion in their defence, to be held at the town hall on 29 January 1523. This was not a true disputation, since the text of the Bible was allowed as the sole authority, and no account was taken of tradition or the laws of the church. The town council staged it rather as a public affirmation of its authority to make changes in religious life and practice. The bishop was fully aware of its propagandist character and did not bother to send a direct representative, although his official Johannes Fabri was present to uphold orthodox views should this be necessary or feasible. Zwingli prepared the Sixty-seven Theses as propositions he was prepared to defend publicly. They contain in summary all of his later teachings, except for the Eucharist, and he later expanded them into an extensive *Commentary on the Sixty-seven Theses.*

1 All who say that the Gospel is invalid without the authority of the church err and slander God.

2 The sum of the Gospel is that our Lord, Jesus Christ, the true son of God, has proclaimed to us the will of his heavenly Father, and has with his sinlessness released us from death and reconciled us to God. 5

3 Therefore, Christ is the only way to salvation for all who ever were, are and shall be.

14 Therefore, all Christian people shall use the greatest diligence that the Gospel of Christ alone be preached everywhere.

15 For in faith rests our salvation, and in unbelief our damnation; for all truth is 10 clear in him.

16 In the Gospel one learns that human doctrines and laws are useless for salvation.

17 [On the pope:] Christ is the only eternal high priest, from which it follows that those who have called themselves high priests have opposed the honour and 15 power of Christ – have, indeed, completely rejected him.

18 Christ, having sacrified himself once and for all, is for all eternity a perpetual and acceptable offering for the sins of all believers, from which it follows that the Mass is not a sacrifice, but is a commemoration of the sacrifice and assurance of the salvation which Christ has given us. 20

19 Christ is the only mediator between God and ourselves.

24 No Christian is bound to do those things which God has not commanded; hence one may eat all food at all times, whence one learns that the dispensations about cheese and butter are a Roman fraud.

25 Time and place are controlled by Christian men and not men by them; hence 25 we learn that those who make rules about time and place deprive Christians of their freedom.

28 All that God has allowed or not forbidden is right; thus, marriage is suitable for all persons.

29 All the so-called clergy sin if they realise that God has denied them the gift of 30 chastity but do not protect themselves by marriage.

31 Excommunication cannot be imposed by any single individual but only by the

church, that is the congregation of those among whom the wrongdoer dwells, in conjunction with their overseer, that is, their minister.

32 Only those who commit public scandal should be excommunicated. 35

34 The pretensions of the so-called spiritual authority have no basis in the teachings of Christ.

35 But the authority and control of the secular power is based on the teaching and actions of Christ.

36 All the rights that the so-called spiritual authority claims belong to secular 40 governments provided they are Christian.

37 All Christians also owe them obedience without exception.

38 In as far as they do not order that which is contrary to God.

39 Therefore all their laws should be in harmony with the divine will, so that they protect the oppressed, even if these do not complain. 45

41 If they give good advice and help to those for whom they must account to God, then these owe them material assistance.

42 But if they are unfaithful and overstep the bounds set by Christ, they may be deposed with God's will.

43 To sum up: that realm is best and most stable which is ruled in accordance 50 with God's will alone, and the worst and weakest is that which is ruled arbitrarily.

Zwingli, *Sämtliche Werke*, vol. 1, pp. 458–63

Questions

1 Compare Zwingli's doctrines with those of Luther as you encountered them in Chapter 1.
2 Were there any substantial disagreements between the two men?
3 What are the implications of Zwingli's views on secular authority?
4 How do they contrast with those of Lutherans?

3.5 Decree establishing evangelical preaching, 29 January 1523

This decree effectively committed Zurich to evangelical reform.

The mayor, Small and Great Council of the city of Zurich, in order to put an end to much disturbance and dissension, have taken counsel and decided . . . that Master Ulrich Zwingli shall continue as before to proclaim the holy Gospel and the pure holy Scripture in accordance with his capabilities, so long and as often as he wishes until something better is made known to him. Furthermore, all people's 5 priests, pastors and preachers in the city, jurisdictions and territories shall undertake to preach nothing but what can be proved by the holy Gospel and the pure holy Scripture. Furthermore they shall in no way for the future slander, abuse or accuse one another as heretics.

Egli, *Actensammlung*, pp. 114–15 (no. 327)

3.6   Statutes of the city of Zurich concerning the clergy and benefices, 29 October 1523

This decree represented the first restructuring of the Zurich church towards a Zwinglian reformation.

In recent days the representatives of the worthy provost and chapter of Sts Felix and Regula appeared before our lord mayor and town council and indicated that out of good will and because of the divine Word . . . they recognised the abuses which they had inherited, but not initiated; with the help of God, these could be changed into a better order of Christian life.   5

First, because all kinds of disturbance might arise . . . because of the tithes, payments and burdens with which the common man claims he is overloaded by the priests, the provost and chapter have agreed to abolish . . . the fees the common folk had to give previously . . . whether for baptisms, prayers, the administration of the Sacraments, requiems or gravedigger's fees, except for headstones. Whoever   10
has or wishes to have a headstone should pay the fees [as before]. Also no one will be forced to have candles for burial, but if anyone wishes to light candles it will be at his own expense. Whoever wishes bells to be tolled for their deceased relatives only in the Great Minster should not have to pay for it, but if they are tolled in the Great Minster and in the other churches, the fee should be paid as is customary.   15

There are a number of clergy here who are idle but still enjoy the usufructs from property, and so it was thought better that the number of priests and clergy should diminish until one has no more than is necessary for the Word of God and other Christian usages.

To the honour of God and for the praise of city and land, an honourable,   20
learned and modest priesthood for the salvation of souls should be set up and maintained in the church of Sts Felix and Regula, so that whenever necessary one can find there men skilled in the Word of God and the Christian life whom one can appoint as pastors, parsons or people's priests for our pious subjects in town and country.   25

Furthermore, the schoolmaster should be more adequately paid than before, so that he may diligently and suitably lead and direct the young boys until they can attend the above-mentioned lessons [in holy Scripture], all without cost to themselves, when the boys are supported at their fathers' expense. They must not be sent out of the city of Zurich or its territory for learning or schooling in foreign   30
parts; rather, they should learn on the spot, without burden to their fathers, not elsewhere in some other schools. For this purpose, we must build suitable lodgings and residence.

When such benefices, offices and ordinances are properly and honourably provided for, what then remains of the dues and rents shall be given to the needy   35
in the hospital, or to the poor folk who reside in the area of the benefice, according to their circumstances. To distribute this to the needy, four persons are to be appointed, namely, two by the provost and chapter and two by the worthy council of the city of Zurich, so that this [distribution of alms] might be done more easily and in orderly fashion. When the time for reappointment of benefices comes   40

around again, all the articles included here are to be read out, and if anyone wants to accept a benefice, he must swear to observe and uphold these articles.

Egli, *Actensammlung*, pp. 169–70 (no. 426)

Questions

1 Summarise the main points covered by this decree.
2 What are the main concerns inspiring the decrees in **3.5** and **3.6**?
3 Why was the council apparently so concerned about questions of finance?
4 How radically did these decrees reform the church in Zurich?
5 How extensive was the town council's control of religion in Zurich as a result?

3.7   Gerold Edlibach's account of the Reformation in Zurich, 1524–6

Edlibach was a conservative Catholic, who died in 1530 at the age of 76. His chronicle notes on the progress of the reforms in Zurich were probably written in the period 1520–6, roughly contemporaneously with the events they describe. He shows how thoroughly religious life was purged of all the elements of traditional cult and worship. The sub-headings have been added by the editors to help the reader gain an overview of the individual stages.

Fasting
Item, one began in Lent of this year [1524] to eat meat, chicken, poultry, eggs and whatever one desired. Whoever did not eat them was mocked, and few folk fasted any more, neither on Quarter days nor on any of the solemn feasts of the Virgin or other solemn feasts, for many people had no fear of excommunication [for breaching the fast]. Many preachers and parsons said fasting was only a bait for the   5
confessional, dreamed up for the sake of cash, and that each person should confess his sins to the lord God in private repentance; that would suffice and one needed no other confession.

The Mass
Item, on the 8 June 1524 my lords of the Great and Small Council of Zurich decreed that the images should be removed from all the churches in the town, its   10
jurisdictions and territories, as well as the crucifixes from the city gates, from the gates of the monasteries and from wherever else they stood. Also in this year, the Mass was abolished, and whatever old priests still celebrated Mass were mocked and despised as 'mass slaves' and 'lord-god-guzzlers' . . . Early morning Masses were hardly celebrated at all. And my lords [the town council] permitted whoever   15
so desired to take home the images [he or his family had founded].

Ceremonies
In these days there were three kinds of Masses celebrated: some distributed
communion without breaking the host [as prescribed in the canon of the Mass, and
which signified Christ's sacrificial death by the breaking of his body]; others
omitted many collects and antiphons, and some observed the Mass as of old. Item,   20
in this year one no longer distributed communion to the sick or gave the last
anointing, unless it was done in secret. Item, the new-born children were only
baptised with water, without holy oil or salt and any other ceremony. Item, no holy
water or salt was blessed on Sundays, and the new-style preachers said they were
useless ceremonies. Item, [the ministers] baptised the children without liturgical   25
vestments, and married couples and proclaimed the Word of God from the pulpit
dressed the same as laymen, and most of them grew long beards like ascetics.

Feast of All Souls and attitudes to the dead
Item, in this year of 1524 the feast of All Souls was forbidden, along with its vigil
and other prayers, and the prayers next morning, whether singing, reading or
celebrating Mass, as well as the visits to the graves of the dead. And very little was   30
donated for the souls of the dead in God's name. These were presented by the
preachers to the common folk as useless ceremonies only pretending to be of use
for the dead.

Images
Now many persons were causing unrest because of images, because the idols had
not been removed from the churches and from roadside shrines, according to the   35
mandate agreed between the town council and the citizens, as noted above. And so
the Great and Small Council agreed once again immediately to remove all images
and idols from all churches, gates and roadside shrines. This was agreed on 15
June 1524, and people were appointed from all the guilds to implement this
decision and mandate of the Small and Great Council. [This was done between 20   40
June and 2 July 1524.] It cannot be denied, as was said at the time, that many of
those deputised to do this work, those from the Great and Small Council excepted,
dealt with the images coarsely and unfittingly, [deeds of] unchristian contempt for
which our forefathers only in recent years had imposed severe penalties.

The 'pew-storm'
The pew-storm in the Great Minster. Now when all the images and idols of the   45
Great Minster were cleared away from the church and the spaces below and stored
in the vaults above the side naves, the minster was reopened. Everyone ran into the
church and each broke up his pewstall in the nave and carried it home. One broke
up this pew, another that, until within half a day all were removed and there were
no more left in the church, and it went on in a rage. That happened on 17 June   50
1524. [The date given here is false, and the correct date is certainly after 2 July.]

The font and shrine
On 8 December 1524 the baptismal font in the Great Minster, which had stood
there for so many hundreds of years that no one could imagine it otherwise, was

broken up . . . On 12 December it was decided by the Great and Small Council
that the tomb of the two martyrs, Sts Felix and Regula, who had long been the   55
city's patron saints [– Zurich was said to have been built on the site of their
martyrdom –], and who were greatly honoured by all men, should be broken up. In
recent years this had been adorned by many pious folk with gilt and costly panels,
and silken cloths covered the coffins in their grave. Twelve lamps had always
burned before them on the vigils of feasts and of Sundays. This tomb was   60
completely broken up. God give them sense.

Abolition of the Mass and the new Lord's Supper
On Monday in Passion Week, 17 April 1525, the Great and Small Council
decreed that from the coming Maundy Thursday no Mass, whether spoken or
sung, should henceforth be celebrated in my lords' town of Zurich, or in its
jurisdictions and territories. And that was passed by a narrow majority. On the   65
Wednesday the last Mass and Passion was celebrated in Zurich and the Mass was
then completely abolished. On the morning of Maundy Thursday the new table of
the Lord was set up, and the bread and wine distributed to the people. That
pleased some, but not others. At the same time an Easter play was performed by
many folk, and an episcopal commission came to Zurich. At the same time many   70
men and women in Zurich received communion according to the old rite, for the
Small and Great Council had allowed the priests to administer it to them for this
year only.

The gravestones
In this year [following a mandate of 18 November 1525] it was announced from
the pulpit that each person had to remove the gravestones from his [family] grave   75
and take them home. If that was not done, the city builder would use them for civic
purposes. Thus the graves of many pious, honourable folk were broken up, torn
apart and abolished, and one may fear that this caused more envy and secret hatred
than charity and love.

Clerical marriage
Item, [on 25 March 1526] it was announced from the pulpits of the three churches   80
within Zurich as a command of the town council that all priests and parsons in the
town would have to take in marriage the housekeepers and maids with whom they
had hitherto scandalously kept house, and lead them to church within fourteen
days on pain of losing their benefices. And there were many young priests who did
so gladly; on the other hand many old and infirm priests were unwilling to do so   85
and many of these left Zurich, giving up their houses and benefices to stand by the
old faith.

Opposition
Item, in this same year there were quite a lot of pious and honourable folk, both
men and women, members of both the Small and the Great Council and from the
Zurich commune who went, some to Einsiedeln, others to Zug, yet others to   90
Baden, Wettingen, Schlieren and Fahr [all places which still upheld the old belief],

in order to celebrate and receive the holy Sacrament on Maundy Thursday, according to the old usage. It was then forbidden by Zurich on pain of a fine for anyone to enter any church in which Mass was celebrated and the old ceremonies were still in force.

95

Bilderstreit. Kulturwandel in Zwinglis Reformation, edited by Hans-Dietrich Altendorf and Peter Jezler, Zurich, 1984, pp. 49–70

Questions

1 What does 3.7 tell us about the various responses and actions of the people of Zurich?
2 How popular did the changes seem to be, judging from this account?
3 What does the writer reveal about his own attitude?
4 For class discussion:
   (a) Why did so many changes take place in quick succession?
   (b) What explanation can you offer for the nature of the changes?

3.8   The formation of a new clerical elite in Zurich, 1523–5

Like Luther and the Wittenbergers, Zwingli very soon abandoned the idea that each person could read and understand the Word of God on their own. Although the Bible was to be the sole standard of doctrine and conduct, it was only to be approached under the guidance of a 'prophet': a preacher, teacher and minister with special linguistic skills and theological learning. Moreover, there was to be no unqualified right of the community to elect its own minister, for he had to be acceptable to the secular authorities and approved by the existing ministers. Although Zwingli seemed to imply that all Christians were potential ministers, this principle seemed to be obscured once arrangements for ministerial training were set up, for Zwingli's 'prophesyings' in the Great Minster became simply a theological college for the training of future pastors. Moreover, given that Zwingli envisaged the duty of such pastors as that of exhorting and warning the civil authorities to govern on Christian principles, a good deal of the old relationship between the secular and the clerical estates was *de facto* re-established. Zwingli's 'prophesyings' provided a model that influenced Calvin's consistory as set up in Geneva, and was imitated in Strassburg. The idea of a group of theologically-informed believers meeting informally formed the prototype of the Puritan 'prophecy' in England, which came to look like a subversive 'church within a church'. The practical upshot of the Zurich prophesyings was the production of the Zurich Bible of 1529, the first complete evangelical translation of the Bible in German.

3.8(a)   *The value of languages in the* Duty of the Preacher, *30 June 1523*

Here [1 Cor. 14] Paul desires that Christians should be instructed in languages, but to the purpose that they should 'prophesy'. Now he well knows that not everyone is skilled in languages, but he shows how useful a thing it would be for Christians to know the languages in which God's Word is written . . . This he wished in order that it might be used advantageously by the prophets, that is, in   5 exposition of the Bible or in preaching.

Zwingli, *Sämtliche Werke*, vol. 4, p. 417

3.8(b)   *Zwingli's advice on Bible lectures, November 1525*

Henceforth on weekdays in summer between 7 a.m. and 8 a.m., and in winter from 8 a.m. a scholar should lecture in the Great Minster on the Bible and Scriptures in three languages, namely Hebrew, Greek and Latin. After each lecture is finished, a preacher is to expound and explain it in German. Zwingli's intention was that those unable to attend the early sermon could attend the later lecture. A preacher   5 would stand on the steps of the choir and explain to the people in German in words they could understand what the scholars had heard in the learned languages. In order that those who come to this same lecture should not be bored too long by languages they did not understand (which would annoy them), a signal should be given when the foreign language part of the lecture ended, so that each   10 new arrival might enter quietly when the German version was started. For if one had to hold the lecture after the sermon, the lecture would be disrupted. One must also consider that some town councillors did not want to sit in the council when trivial matters were being discussed, and so they may sometimes go to hear the sermon (and they sometimes retire there even when weightier matters are being   15 discussed), so that the council sometimes has no quorum. Sometimes, many idle chattering, gossiping women also used to take advantage of the morning interval before and after the sermons to busy themselves with talk and shopping.

Zwingli, *Sämtliche Werke*, pp. 666–7

3.8(c)   *The 'prophesyings'*

Under the papacy prime, terce, sext and nones used to be read in the choir, but now in their place it was arranged that passages from the Holy Bible should be read in their original languages for right and good Christian understanding. This was done at 8 a.m. in the choir, for at the start no lecture room had been built. All this was organised by Zwingli. All the clergy, preachers, canons, chaplains and   5 senior scholars gathered in the choir of the Great Minster occupying the stalls. The first meeting took place in the choir on 19 June 1525, and Master Ulrich Zwingli opened with a prayer.

Then one of the students read out the text from the Bible that was to be expounded. He read it in Latin, since the Bible was then used in Latin translation.   10

They began to read the Bible from the beginning and continued daily throughout the year, with the exception of Sundays and Fridays. When all the books of the Old Testament were completed, they started again from the beginning – they read nothing except the Old Testament. After the student had read out the Latin, Jacob Coeporinus stood up and read the same passage again in Hebrew, for the Old   15
Testament was originally written in Hebrew, and he expounded the Hebrew in Latin. Then Zwingli read the same passage in Greek from the Septuagint and likewise expounded in Latin showing the meaning of the passage in question. Finally, a preacher set out in German what had been said in the other languages, adding a prayer.   20

Bullinger, *Reformationsgeschichte*, vol. 1, p. 290

Questions

1   How would you characterise the nature of the new church as revealed in 3.8(b) and 3.8(c)?
2   What role did laypeople have in this church?
3   Explain the differences between Zwingli's church and that established in Catholic and Lutheran territories (here you may have to consult documents in Chapter 7).

3.9   The town council's decrees on church attendance, 1530–1

By 1530 the reforms in Zurich had progressed to the point where the council was insisting on uniformity, and instituting a policing system to root out heterodoxy. Whether because of Anabaptism or because of lingering attachment to the old belief, church attendance was less than zealous, and the council believed that it was necessary to enforce conformity and outward piety.

26 March 1530: the Kingdom of God is to be sought above all other things. The Word of God is the proper guide for this kingdom and constitutes the true certainty of our salvation. Nonetheless we are informed that some come only occasionally, others virtually not at all, and still others arrive too late to hear the Word of God, thereby offending the church not a little. This is especially the case   5
where there are Anabaptist supporters and adherents. They stand outside before the doors and in the churchyard, or spend the time of the sermon wantonly in inns. Some of them even ridicule and abusively insult the Word of God and its proclaimers. Despite these facts there prevails on the part of the authorities, officials and wardens no attention to God or fear of him. Therefore we earnestly   10
command everyone who resides in our town, jurisdictions or territory, be he of high or low estate, man, woman, child or servant, to attend a service and sermon at least each Sunday at the stated time. Nobody is to evade this order.
    10 August, 1531: the mandate on churchgoing issued last year [1530] has been

poorly observed and people – young and old, men and women – wander idly about, 15
hither and thither, during the sermon time, on the bridges, down the alleys, by the
gates and alongside the moats. Therefore our lords order all persons who bear
responsibility and oversight in the matter of churchgoing [to enforce the
mandate] . . . and hereby earnestly command that every person shall strictly
observe the mandate to attend church on Sundays and holy days. And so that no 20
person may be able fraudently to say that [they have attended elsewhere] the
preachers in all three churches shall begin to preach at one and the same time, a
time convenient to all.

Egli, *Actensammlung*, p. 703 (no. 1656); pp. 760–1 (no. 1780)

Questions

1 What does 3.9 suggest about the attitudes of
  (a) many Zurich citizens to the new arrangements
  (b) the town council to evangelical piety?
2 How effective does the first decree seem to have been?
3 What kind of behaviour was criticised by the town council?
4 Were the problems confined to any single age-group or class?
5 What reasons are given for this behaviour (from the viewpoint of the
  town council)?
6 What response do you think those accused might have given the council?

Jakob Stampfer, Commemorative Silver Medal for Ulrich Zwingli, 1531.
The inscription on the reverse reads: 'Zwingli, the famous scholar and pastor of
Switzerland, you sacrificed yourself on 11 October, and now your soul flies up to
heaven.' Commemorative medals of this kind invoked two sets of associations.
They were a Renaissance fashion, intended to glorify the great and the famous; but
they also recalled the tokens collected at pilgrimage sites which showed the
features of the saint to whom pilgrimage had been made and which were believed
to possess healing powers. It is said that Zwingli's remains were burned and the
ashes scattered by his Catholic opponents to prevent a relic cult growing up. The
issue of a commemorative medal effectively frustrated this intention by glorifying
the Swiss reformer as a saint.

Portrait of Ulrich Zwingli, from Theodore Beza, *Icones* (1580), a collection of
portraits of famous reformers intended to stimulate evangelical devotion.
On a subsequent page, Beza offered the following accompanying description
(original in verse): 'Zwingli burned with a twin love, first of all for God, and then for
his fatherland. He is said to have devoted himself wholly to these two things, first of
all to God and then to his fatherland. How well he pursued his vow to both these
things: he was slain for his fatherland and burned to ashes for his piety.'

4 Reform and rebellion: the German Peasants' War

The purpose of this chapter is not to provide an overview of the causes, political development and military progress of the German Peasants' War, but rather to illustrate the role played in it by evangelical ideas, especially the manner in which the appeal to the Gospel as a standard of social justice led to justification of rebellion. A view of the reactions of theologians and secular authorities to the rebellion also explains much about how the progress of religious reform was shaped in Germany in the years after 1525.

4.1 The rebellion in Upper Swabia: the Baltringen band, February 1525

This document describes a central incident in the course of the rebellion in Upper Swabia, which led to the composition of the Twelve Articles, the major manifesto of the rebels throughout Germany. The account was written by Johannes Kessler of St Gallen some years after the events but almost certainly from information provided by two major participants who had taken refuge there, Christoph Schappeler and Sebastian Lotzer, who were most probably the joint authors of the Twelve Articles.

When the Baltringen peasants began to form bands, the Swabian League's representatives at Ulm sent to the assembled peasants an embassy consisting of a mayor and other prominent men of the town, to ask them what might be the cause and purpose of their gathering. [This was on 9 February 1524.] The mayor spoke to the peasants sharply saying: 'You peasants are like frogs in the spring. You come 5 together and croak "Gwark! Gwark!", and then the stork comes along and swallows you up. You also cry "Woe! Woe!", and the lords [will] come along and strike you dead.'

   At this the leader of the assembly, Ulrich Schmid, stood up and said: 'The assembly which I lead has no intention of causing disturbance or using force, of 10 which we have little. We bear arms and armour not in order to use them, but only to preserve our lives . . . This present assembly has no other complaint . . . than that they are aggrieved beyond measure by you, the lords, in body and in spirit, and

it is impossible for them to bear this any longer. In spirit, because they are robbed
of the Word of God, and so must endure the greatest danger to the salvation of   15
their souls; in body, [because] the assessments and burdens are so fierce and harsh
that neither can be borne by their land or soil. All those here most humbly request
that you will be milder in future.'

The envoys rode off again to Ulm, with the parting message that their lords
would send a reply within a week, whereupon [the assembly] broke up, each   20
looking to himself. When the time for the reply had passed [February 16], the
peasants assembled again thinking that only those who had been there last time
would turn up. But when they tried to order the assembled crowd into companies
of eighty each, they found to their surprise that there were thirty thousand men.
Thus, the disturbance had spread to all parts of Swabia.   25

Now when the League's envoys rode out with their reply and saw the great and
unexpected crowd, each reined in his horse and no one dared to enter the crowd
rashly, for it now looked as though the frogs would eat the stork . . . Thereupon
the embassy requested that the peasants should chose a delegation from the entire
band. When the embassy and the delegation met at the place stated, the mayor   30
gave the [League's] reply in the following words:

'Ulrich Schmid, leader, since you complained a week ago on behalf of the whole
assembly . . . I have been commanded to give no other reply than that the subjects
who complain of burdens from their lords and superiors should take them to law.'

Ulrich Schmid responded: 'Dear lords, God pity you that you should propose   35
recourse to the law for the poor folk who now plead for grace. If it were in their
power to reach agreements with you lords through legal means, then they would
not need all this . . . Their great need, poverty and misery has driven them to it, so
I beg you again that you do not propose going to law, but will show mercy.' Then
the lords went off to one side to think it over a little, but soon returned and said   40
that they would stick by the answer they had given.

At this, Ulrich Schmid asked what law they proposed? They replied, 'the Court
of Chancery', and then they asked what law he proposed. Ulrich replied, 'the
divine law, that pronounces to each estate what it must do or not do'. The lords
replied scornfully: 'Dear Ulrich, you ask for divine law. Tell us who will   45
pronounce on such law? God will hardly come down from heaven and hold a court
session for us!' Ulrich replied: 'Dear lords, it is difficult for me in my simplicity to
indicate judges in a hurry, but I shall do it. I shall take three weeks during which I
shall admonish the priests of every parish to hold public prayers to God that he
might reveal to us learned, pious men to judge this dispute according to the words   50
of divine Scripture.' The lords agreed, with the offer that they would also search
diligently for learned men through public prayer.

**Tom Scott and Bob Scribner (eds.), *The German Peasants' War. A History
in Documents*, Atlantic Highlands, 1991, pp. 123, 126**

Questions

1   Read in class the exchanges in **4.1** as a dialogue or playlet. What does it suggest about:
   (a) the spread of the new evangelical ideas
   (b) the way in which figures such as Luther and other reformers were perceived by both peasants and princes
   (c) the potential role in politics for evangelical reformers?
2   Why did the peasants feel that they had no choice but rebellion?
3   What was the nature of their grievances?
4   Which different notions of the law were used by both sides?
5   Why did the peasants invoke divine law?
6   What did they mean by 'divine law' [**line 44**]?

4.2.   The Christian Union of the peasants of Upper Swabia, March 1525

The most significant organisational form to emerge in the rebellion in south-west Germany was the 'Christian Union' of Upper Swabia, proclaimed on 7 March 1525, following extensive discussion in Memmingen. Its constitution, the 'Federal Ordinance', was drawn up on the same day and, with the Twelve Articles, was one of only two documents from the rebels' side to be printed during the war. The confidence of the peasant rebels in this organisation is reflected in the assured way in which they wrote to such authorities as Archduke Ferdinand.

Committee and envoys of the community in the Allgäu, assembled in Kempten, to Archduke Ferdinand, before 10 March 1525

We beg to inform your Highness as governor and regent of his Roman Imperial Majesty that we poor folk in this land of Allgäu have allied in a Christian union, for the praise of Almighty God, the holy Gospel and the furtherance of the Word of God and the succour of divine law, and for the augmentation of the common Public Peace which the Almighty has left upon earth, and in the interests of   5 brotherly love.

   Such a Christian union intends no vexation or disadvantage to your Highness as archduke of Austria or to other princes, lords, counts, barons, knights, noblemen or anyone, as divine law shows. For what we poor folk are obliged by divine law to perform for your Highness as our gracious territorial prince and governor, as well   10 as for [other] spiritual and temporal authorities, we will in no way oppose or resist, but perform obediently.

   Since we poor folk desire nothing other than divine law and it is not our mind and intention to do violence to anyone, it is our most humble submission and plea to your Highness as governor and regent of the Roman Emperor, as a lover of   15 justice and as the ground, source and protector of divine law, that your Highness as governor will graciously protect, defend and support us poor folk with the divine law.

Scott and Scribner, pp. 129–30

Questions

1 How would the authorities view the statements in this letter?
2 What had led to the formation of the 'Christian Union'?
3 What were the purposes of the 'Christian Union'?
4 Why might it be seen as a revolutionary organisation?

4.3   The Word of God as political principle

The rebellion broke out because many peasants were convinced that they could not secure a just hearing for their grievances by recourse to legal procedures. The introduction of evangelical ideas by preachers and layfolk produced what was almost a revolutionary political principle: the Word of God, as contained in the Old and New Testaments, as a means of adjudging what was just in Christian society. The county of Klettgau belonged to Count Rudolf von Sulz, but stood under the protection of the city of Zurich. Around New Year 1525 the Klettgauers drew up articles of grievance in which they put forward godly justice as the sole guiding principle by which their obligations to Count Rudolf should be adjudged. However, the grievances raised no objection to feudal lordship as such.

They should negotiate in no other way than according to the only benchmark for justice, that is, according to the Word of God, and should have no other judge nor commit themselves to negotiations, unless the Old and New Testaments be [allowed as] judges. For there is no truer judge in heaven or on earth than the Word of God, and all our affairs and concerns, life and being consist only in   5
the Word of God and not in the inconstancy and vanity of mankind. The same living Word will be our judge. That is the opinion of the entire county of Klettgau and the power [of attorney] that we have given our emissaries for negotiation.

Scott and Scribner, pp. 251–2

Questions

1 On what basis do the peasants speak out so fearlessly in **4.2** and **4.3**? How would you characterise their demands and attitude?
2 Read carefully the introduction to **4.3**, noticing what it says about the revolutionary principle underlying the peasants' actions. Pick out some statements from **4.2** and **4.3** which illustrate this principle.

3   On what basis were the emissaries asked to negotiate with their lord?
4   What response were they likely to evoke from
    (a) Count Rudolf von Sulz
    (b) the city of Zurich (consult **4.7**)?

4.4   The role of radical preachers in the rebellion

Besides better-known figures such as Thomas Müntzer (see **6.4–6.5**), many idealistic and militantly radical preachers supported the peasants' cause.

4.4(a)   *Charges laid against Hans Fischer, preacher at Vipiteno (Sterzing), 27 April 1526*

On Palm Sunday [25 March] there were many peasants, two tables full of them, at Peter Kurssner's [house] in Sterzing and they sent for the preacher, who told them that their oath [of allegiance] and whatever they had sworn to their territorial prince was not valid before God, and that they should not be at all concerned at not keeping it. And the Mass was of no value – the priests merely practised sorcery   5
in it. He also said that the Sacrament, which is kept reserved in the church for consoling the sick was of no value, and snapped his fingers with great disrespect.

He abused the king, electors and princes before the citizens and peasants, and called them fools, dolts, braggards and blind folk . . . and related how the Greeks and the Swiss had expelled their princes and nobles and they now held and ruled   10
their lands for themselves. He gave the citizens and peasants grounds for being disobedient to the nobility. And the peasants said among themselves, what should we do, how are we to attack?

The renegade Dominican on this occasion left them with these words: 'Alas, I warrant that there are scarcely ten good and proper believing Christians in the   15
whole town.' He preached that if the territorial prince did not justify going to war, the commons should give no aid, and thus he incited them to disobedience. At the time of the consecration in the Mass, he screwed up his mouth at the holy Sacrament.

4.4(b)   *A parson desires community of goods*

There were many calls during the rebellion for a radical redistribution of property, sometimes justified by reference to the norms of the Gospel. We rarely find an attempt being made to put this into practice, as did Jorg Mentz, the pastor of Neuler in the ecclesiastical territory of Ellwangen, to the evident embarrassment of the watching peasants.

Thomas Opfferkirch: said that on the first summons [to rise and join the rebels] he heard from the parson, the reverend Jorg Mentz, in his (the parson's) house that the summons and the affair were a fraternal matter and they should share one with

another; whereupon he [the parson] threw his keys upon the table and said to Veit
Eberhart he should unlock and share out the parson's goods, and afterwards they   5
would all go from house to house, and whoever had more than another should
share it out with them; and there were ten of them present as he spoke these
words.

Hans Mayer, miller in Schlierbach: said that on the evening when the first
summons came . . . he had come from Ellwangen to the parson's house for the   10
rendering of the annual parish accounts, a meeting of the commune had been
called, and the parson's room was bursting at the seams; among other things, the
parson told several of them: well now, he understood full well that they all must be
equal and share what they had one with another; then he took his keys out of his
pocket and threw them on the table, declaring that he and others should begin at   15
once to share out [his goods] in his house, but no one wanted [to touch] the keys.
Whereupon he, the miller, left the village, returned to his mill and slept at home
that night. He thought that it would not have gone so badly in Neuler if the parson
and Mulhanlin had not been there.

Scott and Scribner, pp. 106–8.

Questions

1   Why were charges brought against the 'renegade Dominican' [4.4 (a),
    line 14] Hans Fischer?
2   Were his offences more political than religious?
3   What happened when the pastor of Neuler tried to take literally the
    demand for community of goods?
4   What does this incident reveal about peasant attitudes towards the
    events of the Peasants' War?

4.5   Articles of the town of Münnerstadt, *circa* 21 April 1525

The rebellion was as much made by discontented artisans of small towns in
most regions of Germany as by the peasantry, Moreover, in central
Germany such towns played a leading role, expounding ideas and grievances typified by this document. Münnerstadt was a territorial town subject
to the joint rule of Wilhelm von Henneberg and the bishop of Würzburg.
Its call for equality of the sexes in education was almost unique at this time.
For the sake of brevity, only a few of the nineteen articles are reproduced
here.

   1 Henceforth the office of preacher and proclaimer of the Word of God is to be
[one] elected by the Christian community and assembly of Münnerstadt, which
shall have power to elect and dismiss preachers and pastors as often as there is
need and it so pleases them.

2 Therefore the ways of priests and monks as they have hitherto been practised 5
shall no longer be tolerated or allowed, but two eminent, upright and learned men
shall be elected to preach according to the teaching of Paul, and to proclaim the
Word of God. These two shall perform their office diligently and truly. And . . .
two men shall be appointed as Levites [i.e. deacons], who shall maintain and look
after a public school, in which the children of all citizens shall be taught free of 10
charge, . . . and where they will be diligently instructed in the Christian Gospels,
so that each child will be the better prepared for a trade or other suitable
employment, according to his ability, also that we may gain from them preachers
and proclaimers of the Word of God who are skilled in Scripture.

3 If such preachers and teachers should in time embark upon the estate of 15
marriage, their wives, who will be of upright, honorable and Christian life, may be
directed to teach the girls who are sent there and to instruct them in Scripture, so
that both the male and the female sex, created equal by God, may the better know
the laws and faith.

Scott and Scribner, p. 177

Questions

1   Summarise the aims of the town of Münnerstadt. How do they
    compare with the principles expressed in 4.2?
2   In what respects are the Münnerstadt Articles 'radical'? What social
    changes are proposed and on what grounds?
3   What role is suggested for women in the new church organisation?
4   How do the good intentions expressed here compare with the
    experience of new pastors as described in 4.4(a), 4.4 (b) and 2.13 [line
    18]?

4.6   Philip Melanchthon's judgement on the Twelve Articles

As a result of negotiations with his rebellious peasants in May 1525, the
Elector Palatine sought an opinion from the leading preacher in Württemberg, Johannes Brenz, and from Melanchthon in Wittenberg.
Melanchthon's reply was composed in the second half of May or the first
week of June, and printed in August or September 1525. Although
Melanchthon broadly agreed with Luther in condemning the rebellion, his
tone was more moderate. For the sake of brevity, Melanchthon's views on
only a few of the key articles have been excerpted here.

Since the peasants invoke the holy Gospel and use it as an excuse, it is necessary to
know what the holy Gospel demands from us or does not . . . Now they claim that
they wish to be instructed by the Gospel, so it is fair that they are presented with
the Gospel and proper Christian teaching, for without doubt there are many in the

peasant bands who sin out of ignorance, and one hopes that if they are properly   5
instructed they will be able to refrain from such felonious deeds and consider
God's judgement, their souls and their poor wives and children.

On the tithe. The tithe is not rendered by virtue of the Old Testament, for we
are no longer bound by that, but by virtue of secular laws and government
concerning how property is distributed. For Paul says, Romans 13:7, pay taxes to   10
whom taxes are due . . . But you say, the lords do not use these things properly, the
monks and priests enjoy them and do nothing for them. The reply is: what has that
to do with you? For you should take nothing away from the authorities, and
whatever is imposed upon you you should render to those appointed to receive it
until the authorities decide otherwise. You act rightly thus, since to take something   15
from someone by force is a felony.

On serfdom. It is also a felony and an act of violence that they do not want to be
serfs. But they bring in Scripture, saying that Christ has made us free, although
this is said of spiritual freedom, namely that we are certain that our sins are taken
away through Christ without us giving satisfaction for them . . . Christian freedom   20
resides in the heart and cannot be seen with fleshly eyes. Outwardly a Christian
patiently and joyously endures secular and civil laws and uses them like food and
drink, be he serf or subject, nobleman or ruler.

Conclusion: first, the peasantry are wrong and act contrary to God in rebelling
and using violence against their authorities, for even if all the articles were quite   25
correct, God still demands obedience to rulers, as St Paul says, Romans 13:2,
whoever resists the authorities will be punished.

Second, . . . the peasants act unchristianly by cloaking themselves in the name of
the Gospel, and the devil has incited the peasants to this for the sole purpose of
abusing and slandering the holy Gospel, and has introduced a delusion about faith,   30
which obscures the Gospel as it was before.

Third, it is unjust to incite disturbance even if the articles were all just, for one
should yield to authority. Now the majority of the articles are unjust, so that it is
pitiful that the blind folk place their wives and children, their own bodies and souls
in danger for such petty reasons.   35

Fourth, I beg the princes first of all to undertake amicable discussions, and to
moderate whatever can fairly be conceded . . . Now when God has granted victory
and the murderous hordes who desire to accept no peace come to be punished, the
princes should show moderation, so that no injustice is done to the innocent.

**A. Laube and H. W. Seifert (eds.), *Flugschriften der Bauernkriegszeit*,
Berlin, 1975, pp. 223–41 *passim***

Questions

1   How do Melanchthon's conclusions answer or contradict the earlier
    demands of the peasants (in 4.1 and 4.2) based on the Gospel?
2   How does he dismiss their demands on the tithe and on serfdom?
3   What is Melanchthon's attitude to authority? Compare this with
    Luther's (4.9).

4   What practical suggestions does Melanchthon make to the Elector about reforming the church?
5   Why does he place so much emphasis on education?
6   What criticism does he make of the peasants' conduct during the revolt? How does he explain their actions? How does he suggest the rebels should be treated?

4.7   Zurich, the Gospel and the tithe

The Zurich peasants were also involved in disturbances in 1524–5, especially on the question of the tithe. The account here is drawn from Johannes Stumpf's 'Reformation Chronicle', written in the 1530s. Stumpf was active as a Zwinglian preacher from 1522, especially in the Zurich uplands, so that he witnessed most of the events he described. He also had access to the Zurich city archives, from which he copied many original documents to incorporate in his chronicle.

The town council issued a mandate on 14 August 1525, stating: 'Since we heard, saw and felt that there were some who, out of self-seeking, persisted in their disobedience, from which great disadvantage might ensue for us and all of you in the eyes of God, our fellow Confederates and other neighbors on our borders who receive tithes in our territories, so we nominated certain councillors and biblical   5
scholars to read through and search the holy Scripture with especial diligence and industry. And we can find in no part of the divine Word . . . that anyone is obliged either to give the tithe or to refuse it. Thus, it is unfitting for us or any judge to refuse any holders, ecclesiastical or lay, their tithes where they have been rendered and received in peaceful possession for many hundreds of years according to   10
praiseworthy ancient tradition and good credentials, and thus to take their property from them.'

The council ordered that the great and small tithe be paid as before, while promising some concessions on the small tithe. They also promised to restore the proper use of the tithe according to the Word of God.

The peasants were not at all content with this explanation or in agreement with it. They had promised [earlier] that they would commit their lives and goods for the Word of God, [believing that] their evangelical freedom would bring them some advantage. Many took the tithe into their own barns and were later punished for it. They laid all the blame for this on the preachers, since some of them were said to   15
have proclaimed that the tithe was not demanded in the New Testament. [They now said that] since they were ancient traditions, usages and customs bequeathed to us, no Christian should refuse to pay them, but give the cloak as well as the coat. But this proposal vexed the peasants, who withdrew in great hatred of the preachers, where previously they would have given their right arm for the Gospel.   20

Scott and Scribner, pp. 111–13

Questions

1   What was the composition of the meeting described in **4.7**? What reason was given by the authorities for the continuation of the tithe? What final decision was made?
2   What does this document reveal about the motives of the peasants in becoming followers of evangelical teaching?
3   Why did the peasants become so incensed against the preachers?

4.8   Justification of rebellion

The anonymous pamphlet *To the Assembly of Common Peasantry* was probably written in Upper Swabia at the end of April or the beginning of May 1525 and appeared in print shortly afterwards. It provided a consistent argument justifying rebellion of subjects against unjust lords on the basis of precedents drawn from biblical and classical sources. Its author emphasises communal government and the need for rulers to act in the practical interests of brotherly love, and does not support capricious rebellion. This places it close to Zwinglian ideas on government and social ethics.

Dear brothers in Christ, you know that the Lord says 'render to Caesar the things which are Caesar's' . . . [Matthew 22:21] – just as he himself paid the tribute to Caesar, Matthew 17:24–7 . . . Therefore we are obliged . . . to obey our rulers . . . But [tyrants] certainly give quite a different meaning [to the texts on obedience] for they stretch the scope of obedience too far, making a painted idol out of it . . . Yea, 5 they have certainly engaged in much banging and thumping about their authority and power based on the above-mentioned scriptural passage, but God has hitherto not enlightened them with his grace so that they can recognize what true authority is. This would be tolerable if they did not turn authority into a manic frenzy.

Indeed, [this was] the first cause and origin of the entire Swiss Confederation, 10 which removed tyrannical power from the nobility and their other rulers who without mercy and contrary to all justice had every day forced and coerced the common man with unchristian tyrannical rapine rooted in their own pride, criminal power and enterprise. That had to be abolished and rooted out through much war, bloodshed and use of the sword, as is related in the Swiss chronicles 15 and in many other reliable histories.

Whether a community may depose its authority: Now for the matter! Trust to God! Now the alarm bells will sound! The truth must come out now . . . All those lords who, out of the desire of their hearts and their evil and wilful heads, selfishly arrogate to themselves – I will not say plunder – taxes, customs and excise and 20 whatever may serve the common purse for the protection and maintenance of the common territory, these are the true thieves and declared enemies of their country.

And the first saying from godly law is as follows: Joshua 1:7ff commands that no

lord should have the power to act according to his own will, but only from godly
law, otherwise he shall be driven out, which is the most pleasing to God. The   25
second [saying from] godly law is spoken to us by St Paul in 2 Corinthians 10:8,
where he says that power is given for edification, not for destruction. And what
does St Paul mean by this injunction other than that harmful rulers should not be
tolerated.

The third divine jurist, St Luke, writes [Luke 13:6–9] about the barren tree,   30
which should be cut down so that the entire land will not be ruined . . . From
which nothing follows and there is no other interpretation than that when an entire
country has for a long time suffered the arbitrariness and ruin of its lord, hopes
that he will show some improvement and if he will not, then the common
countryside should boldly arm itself with the sword, Luke 17:1ff, and say: 'We are   35
no longer obliged to this disloyal steward and evil lord'. This view is described for
us in Luke 12:[41–8] . . . Are they not all clear divine sayings against godless
authority, which is not to be tolerated, but to be deposed without timidity? Nor may
any lip-serving Christians say 'The Gospel is not concerned with the secular
sword.' Their hearts are false and damnable, for they boast that they are servants   40
of God by virtue of Romans 13.

Subjects have never rebelled against any Christian lord who has ruled well. It
has always happened under the wastrels and godless tyrants. Scripture is full of
evidence, and especially Moses. Although he was to have been a future king of
Egypt, nonetheless he took pity on the poor people under the great tyrant Pharoah   45
and raised a Poor Conrad against him [an allusion to the peasant revolt in
Württemberg in 1514], and repudiated his royal dignity. And in what unspeakable
fear, need and misery did he place himself with the poor people, until he redeemed
them from the tyrants [cf Exodus 3:7–12].

Yea, they scream, curse and revile the rebellion so evilly, and want to damn it   50
totally, and never think thereby about the cause of the disturbance, which is
themselves and their godless being. Be proud of your *Bundschuh*. Even if the lords
drone on and on, and put forward their ancient customs, and present their case
suavely, don't be fooled . . . when one has acted unjustly for a thousand years, that
would never be right for a single hour.   55

Scott and Scribner, pp. 269–76

Questions

1 How does the writer indicate that he favours authority if properly used?
2 How does he go on to suggest that '[tyrants] . . . stretch the scope of
   obedience too far' [**line 5**]? What characterises a tyrant in his view?
3 What criteria does he set out for deciding 'whether a community may
   depose its authority' [**line 17**]?
4 How far does the writer justify rebellion on the basis of the Word of God?
5 Explain the references to 'the entire Swiss Confederation' [**line 10**]
   and to the '*Bundschuh*' [**line 52**].

4.9   Luther's intervention in the rebellion and his reaction

In April 1525 Luther, on his own initiative, undertook a tour through the Mansfeld Valley and Thuringia, preaching to the rebellious peasantry in the hope of pacifying the revolt. He was not well received and his preaching had no effect. It seems, however, to have fixed in his mind the idea that the peasants were all violent and murderous rogues who should be shown no mercy. The first letter here was written towards the end of his journey, to a kinsman on his mother's side, and reveals the immediate impression he formed under the influence of his hostile reception.

4.9(a)   *Luther to Johann Rühel, councillor of the counts of Mansfeld, 4 May 1525*

Honoured, dear doctor and kinsman. During this entire trip I have constantly been mulling over the news [about the rebellion] which you told me in parting; therefore I must write to you now about this matter.

To begin with, I urge you not to influence my gracious lord, Count Albrecht, to be soft in this affair . . . For we have God's Word, which does not lie; it says in   5 Romans 13, [4]: 'He does not bear the sword in vain,' etc . . . Therefore as long as there is life in him, his Grace ought to use his sword to punish the wicked . . . As a result his Grace may have a good conscience, and until death pursue and be dedicated to the duties of his office for the sake of God's Word.

If there were thousands more of the peasants, they would still be altogether   10 robbers and murderers, who take the sword simply because of their own insolence and wickedness, and who want to expel sovereigns and lords, to destroy everything, and to establish a new order in this world. But for this they have neither God's commandment, authority, right or injunction, as the lords have it now. Besides, the peasants are faithless and are committing perjury toward their lords. Above all this,   15 they borrow the authority of the divine Word and Gospel to cover up their great sins, and thus disgrace and slander God's name.

It is a mockery on the devil's part when the peasants pretend that they do not hurt or harm anyone. Is it not doing harm when they drive out and kill their lords? If they do not wish to hurt anyone, why do they gather in hordes and insist that one   20 yield to their demands? To hurt one and yet to take everything – that's the way the devil would do good and hurt no one, if one would let him do as he pleases. Pure insolence is the only reason for driving out their lords. Why does one not rather improve what is wrong [with the system]? Look at the government of the S. [i.e. the Swiss]. It also began this way, and is now worse than it has ever been. There is no   25 discipline or obedience among the S., and they are nothing but mercenaries.

I (for whom this is also intended, since the devil definitely wants to have me dead) am well aware that the devil is angry, since up to now he has been unable to accomplish anything by fraud or force. He is set to get rid of me, even if he has to attempt the worst and confound the whole world altogether. I almost believe and 30 think that it is because of me that the devil is making such a mess in the world . . . Well, if I get home I shall prepare for death with God's help, and await my new lords, the murderers and robbers, who tell me they will not harm anyone.

WA Briefwechsel, vol. 4, pp. 479–82

4.9(b) *Luther to Nicolaus von Amsdorf, 30 May 1525*

Nicolaus von Amsdorf was one of Luther's most admiring disciples. He wrote to Luther from Magdeburg, expressing his concern about the bad reputation Luther had gained by his tract against the peasants, especially the hostile reactions of some of the towns' evangelical preachers. Characteristically, Luther interprets this as another attack on him by the devil.

Grace and peace! You inform me of a new honour, my Amsdorf, namely that I am called a toady to the princes. Satan has conferred many such honorary titles on me in these years. But I will not deplore such know-alls, who in judging me only betray their own bloodthirsty and seditious spirit. Rejoice, then, that Satan is indignant and blasphemes whenever I touch him. For what are these but the voices of Satan, 5 by which he tries to traduce me and the Gospel?

Indeed, I think that it is better that all the peasants should be killed rather than that the princes and magistrates should be destroyed, because the peasants take up the sword without God's command. What iniquity of Satan can follow from this but the complete satanic devastation of the kingdom of God and the world. Even if 10 the princes act excessively at least they bear the sword at God's command. Under them it is still possible for the two kingdoms to exist. However, the peasants deserve no mercy or patience, but rather the wrath and indignation of God and man. For they did not comply when they were warned, nor yield when even the fairest terms were offered to them, but continued to confound everything with the 15 rage of Satan, as those in Thuringia and Franconia did. To excuse them, to show them mercy or to favour them would be to deny and blaspheme God, and to wish to eject him from heaven. Tell this to those preachers of yours who may attempt or dare [to excuse the peasants], but I will never consent to it. Indeed, I will curse their efforts in the name of the Lord. Afterwards the Lord will judge which spirit is 20 from the devil, theirs or mine. But I am grieved that we have handed over the office of the Word and its reputation to such blasphemous people. May God instruct and convert them or depose them from their seats again. Amen. Farewell in the Lord.

WA Briefwechsel, vol. 4, pp. 517–18

Questions

1   How does Luther characterise the peasants in these two passages?
2   What advice does he pass on to the count of Mansfeld through his kinsman Rühel?
3   To what extent does it seem that Luther really has become a 'toady to the princes' [**4.9(b), line 2**]?
4   It is often suggested that Luther kept much of the medieval outlook of his upbringing. What light is cast on this by **4.9(a)** and **4.9(b)**?
5   Can you suggest why Luther felt so strongly against rebellion?
6   Using quotations, compare **4.8** and **4.9** in the attitudes they express towards rulers and ruled.
7   Compare Luther's views on the Swiss with those of the author of **4.8**.

4.10   The consequences of Luther's stance

The shocked reactions even of Luther's closest supporters to his denunciation of the peasants is reflected in this letter from a prominent Lutheran, Hermann Mühlpfort, mayor of Zwickau, one of the earliest towns to adopt religious reforms – Luther had dedicated his 1520 tract *On Christian Liberty* to Mühlpfort. Mühlpfort's views here are coloured by typical urban hostility to the nobility, while ignoring the role of towns such as Zwickau in provoking peasant grievance.

Hermann Mühlpfort to Stephan Roth at Wittenberg, 4 June 1525
Doctor Martin has fallen into great disfavour with the common people, also with both learned and unlearned; his writing is regarded as having been too fickle. I am greatly moved to write to you about this, for the pastor [Nikolaus Hausmann] and the preachers here have been greatly disconcerted and amazed by the tracts   5
recently issued, since one is clearly contrary to the other. First, [in his *Admonition to Peace: a Reply to the Twelve Articles of the Peasants in Swabia*] that Christian man Dr Martin certainly wrote well, addressing both sides about the danger of princes and peasants jeopardising their souls' salvation; with God's grace, he certainly expressed a sound judgement with his proposal about how the matter could be   10
mediated, for I, with my limited understanding, knew of no better counsel.
     Afterwards, in a second tract [*A Shocking History and God's Judgement on Thomas Müntzer*] written after he had received a letter from Thomas Müntzer, who so pitiably misled the poor folk, he [Luther] became instead the hammer of the poor, without regard for their need, by calling for the poor alone to be quickly destroyed.   15
In the third tract [*Against the Robbing and Murdering Hordes of Peasants*], which I do not consider theological, he called for the private and public murder of the peasants: as long as strength coursed through one's veins, they should be sent to their judgement before God. Is the devil, and those who do this, to be our Lord God? Here I do not agree. In my opinion, there was no pressing need for this rash   20

tract. There was enough murdering of peasants, burghers, women and children taking place; not only were the poor folk being killed, but also their goods and possessions were being taken from their innocent wives and children and burnt. God knows, these same knights are supposed to be the children of God! But we should have more pity for the poor, needy and simple folk who were misled by　　25 Thomas and others, and when Thomas Müntzer's letter arrived, [Luther] might well have reacted more thoughtfully.

It is true, as Martin writes, that rebellion should be put down, and it is entirely fitting that secular authority should punish, though they do it without being asked; but, contrary to his first tract, he conceded too much to one side – indeed, far too　　30 much, for the poor were to be strangled. I find that incomprehensible. I know what is happening in towns and villages, such that one should complain to God in heaven . . . But Martin's remedy is said to be the best: that the peasants should bear more, while the nobility [receive] the lion's share and yet concede the least . . . See how violently the nobility will impose all their burdens on the people　　35 with the sword and [shed] the blood of the suffering poor, who cannot protect themselves from hunger because of their poverty. But they [the nobility] will rely on Martin's tract, that this will gain them eternal salvation. If my gracious lord [the elector of Saxony] and other princes had issued a public edict calling for regard for the need of the peasantry, and they had not then disbanded, I would not have had　　40 so much pity, but no such thing happened.

Dear Christian brother, who will now speak out about the need of the commons in town and village? Who will have the strength of spirit not to hold back from doing so? Whoever speaks out will be accused of being a rebel and everyone will have to keep silent for fear of tyrants, lest it be said that one is speaking against　　45 authority. I know already that in several places more has been imposed upon the poor than before and they are told openly: 'You owe me this; if you do not do it, you are opposing me, who am your lord and have sovereign authority over you.' It is said that complaints should be laid before the princes; [but] yea, I know no one [who] will be a just judge . . . I know of matters that were complained about forty　　50 years ago; what has been achieved other than trouble, care, labour and expenditure of money? Christ's sheep must suffer and leave things to God. The poor lack instruction because they are provided with poor preachers.

Scott and Scribner, pp. 322–4

Questions

1　Summarise the development of Luther's views as given here by Mühlpfort.
2　What reservations does Mühlpfort express in his comments on Luther's 'rash tract' [**lines 20–1**]?
3　What justifications does he offer for Luther's views?
4　Why is he so pessimistic about the long-term consequences of the Peasants' War?

5   In the last two paragraphs, what regrets does the writer express about the outcome of the war and future conditions?
6   What was the wider significance of the views and reactions of Luther as expressed in these documents and others, such as that entitled *Against the Robbing and Murdering Hordes of Peasants?*

4.11   Margraves Casimir and George of Brandenburg: edict on the preaching of the Gospel, 30 August 1525

This edict reflects what quickly became the stock Lutheran interpretation of the rebellion, that the peasants had been led astray by false preachers, the chief of whom was Thomas Müntzer. The princes' response was to emphasise their subjects' duty of unconditional obedience and to take stronger control over preaching to ensure that unsuitable preachers could not stir up future trouble. It also reflects concern about popular interpretation of the new doctrines of 'Christian freedom'.

The recent rebellion and disturbance arose for the most part because of unlearned and unsuitable preachers . . . It is the command of lords Casimir and George, as margraves of Brandenburg, . . . that in their princely graces' lands all such preachers should be at once removed . . . Where one or more is encountered (who has publicly preached . . . rebellion contrary to the holy Gospel) . . . these should   5
be arrested immediately and punished earnestly and remorselessly, . . . or exiled from the land.
   Much misunderstanding has arisen from what was previously preached for a time, [namely] that faith alone in God and Jesus Christ is sufficient for the attainment of eternal blessedness, which is true when this is a proper and living   10
faith in the depths of the heart. But many coarse and simple men have thought and said that if faith alone is sufficient, there is then no need to do good works, as if a right, true, loving faith in God our Lord could exist without good works.
   So all preachers in the lands of my gracious lords are herewith commanded that when they preach that faith alone is sufficient for salvation they should always   15
explain that it is not a bad, false, dead faith (as the poor, coarse or simple man believes), but a true, living, loving and charitable faith, from which at all times rightful good works (that is those commanded by God) towards God and one's neighbor must of necessity follow . . . But some unskilled preachers did not explain all this with sufficient discrimination, from which the common man   20
derived a misunderstanding, as though Christians were not obliged to perform temporal duties for their authorities but that they were freed from this because of divine law (from which no little disturbance has followed).
   All preachers in the lands of my gracious lords are herewith earnestly commanded that when they preach henceforth about Christian freedom they   25
should each time explain and indicate to the people in good German words what

true Christian freedom is . . . and that Christian freedom resides in the spirit and not in the flesh.

From clear and powerful sayings of divine and holy Scripture it is surely sufficiently shown that Christian freedom does not consist in the removal of rents, interest, dues, tithes, taxes, services or other similar external burdens, but is only an inward and spiritual thing, as said above, and that all subjects are obliged to obey their authorities in such temporal business, affairs, and commands. All preachers should truly explain and indicate that to the people as often as they preach or speak about Christian freedom, so that the subjects will not be misled from a right, true and Christian freedom of the spirit into a devilish, unchristian freedom of the flesh, and so be brought to lose their soul, body, life, honor and goods, as unfortunately happened many times in this rebellion.

If ever the preachers say on the basis of Scripture that some useless persons do not receive their revenues justly from the community (as has hitherto often been said and written), it is not to be understood from this that subjects may with force and by direct action resist giving or performing these same traditional temporal usufructs, from which a revolt may follow, for in each case they should always add: that although a secular authority or someone else may take traditional usufructs unjustly from the people, yet the subjects may not oppose this with any violent or rebellious deed, but must commend it to the judgement of God, just as every true Christian must endure injustice, but should not do injustice.

Scott and Scribner, pp. 330–1

Titlepage to the Twelve Articles
(1525).
The woodcut illustration shows
a typical gathering of peasants,
perhaps in a room at an inn or
private house, to discuss their
grievances and what to do about
them.

Questions

1 What seems to have been the main anxiety of the princes who issued this edict?
2 What are the two different meanings of 'freedom' which they identify?
3 Why are they so anxious to promote their view that 'Christian freedom resides in the spirit and not in the flesh' [**lines 27–8**]?
4 What further problem might arise among the peasants who accept 'Christian freedom'?

Pamphlet condemning Luther's stance in the German Peasants' War.
Luther's condemnation of the peasants played into the hands of Catholic
opponents, such as the author of this pamphlet, the Franciscan Johannes Findling,
who piled up fifty-five 'expressions of amazement' about Luther's behaviour at the
time.

5 Two Reformation controversies

I: The problem of images

Images very quickly became a central issue of the reform movements, partly because they were so closely associated with the cult of the saints, pilgrimages and miraculous shrines, but also because of their central role in the Catholic liturgy. They were linked to many popular beliefs, which reformers such as Zwingli condemned as superstitious and idolatrous, and were suspected of moving devout laypeople to worldly rather than spiritual feelings. However, they also focused a wide range of other issues: greater access of the rich to salvation by works, the misapplication of communal wealth to material objects instead of to 'the living images of Christ', the poor. The problem of how to deal with images quickly became one which radically divided the reform movements, the main division arising between conservative Lutherans and more radical evangelical thinkers such as Zwingli, Carlstadt and the Anabaptists. This was not merely a disagreement about theology, but also about how to acquire knowledge of the divine. Those such as Luther emphasised the educational value of images and the impossibility of thinking about salvation without images; those such as Zwingli or Carlstadt mistrusted human emotions and emphasised the need for religion to work through the spirit. It was also an issue involving questions of practical action. Zealous evangelical believers, impatient with temporising authorities, often took the law into their own hands and smashed images. For some the orderly removal of images was sufficient, for others it became a symbolic action, signifying their liberation from the old faith. Indeed, for some evangelical believers, the breaking of images could almost become a form of counter-magic, testing whether the images did possess any sacred power, as held in traditional popular belief.

5.1 The pre-Reformation view of images

The reformers' reaction to images cannot be understood without some reference to late-medieval ideas about the role of images in popular piety.

Images are made for three reasons. The first is for the sake of the unlearned, so
that if they cannot read writing they can read from the walls. The second is
because of the sluggishness of human emotions, which cannot be moved from
their sloth to devotion in other ways, yet which may be aroused by viewing images.
The third is because of forgetfulness, so that when we forget what we have heard   5
we may recall it though seeing.

Preceptorium deutsch (1452)

5.2   Carlstadt, *On the Abolition of Idols*, 1522

That we keep images in church and in God's house is not right and contrary to the
First Commandment 'Thou shalt have no strange gods.' The houses of God are
houses wherein God alone is honoured, prayed to and invoked. As Christ says, my
house is a house of prayer but you have made it a pit of murderers. Deceitful
images murder all those who praise and pray to them . . . We cannot even deny   5
that we have erected the so-called saints in the churches out of love, for if we did
not love them, we would not have set them up where God alone should reside and
rule . . . Have we not shown them the honour which we show and render to great
lords? Why have we clothed them in velvet and damask, painted and coloured
them in silvered and gilded clothing? Why have we bedecked them with golden   10
crowns and precious stones?

    But [Pope] Gregory says: the laity should use images for books. Tell me, dear
Gregory, or have someone else tell me: what can the laity ever learn from images?
You must admit that one learns merely fleshly life and suffering from them, and
that they lead no further than to the flesh, and they can bring you no further.   15
Example: from the image of the crucified Christ you will learn nothing other than
the fleshly suffering of Christ, how Christ bowed his head and the like . . . Now
images are dumb and deaf, can neither see nor hear, neither learn nor teach, and
signify nothing other than mere plain flesh, and that is of no use; and so it follows
that they are of no use . . . Thus it is not true that images are the books of the   20
common folk, for they learn no salvation from them.

Carlstadt, *Von Abtuung der Bilder*, 1521

5.3   Luther on images, 1525

I have also attacked image-breaking, for images should first be torn out of the
heart through the Word of God and despised and rejected, as happened well
before Dr Carlstadt dreamed of iconoclasm. For once they are removed from the
heart, they do no harm to the eyes. But Dr Carlstadt, who cares nothing about the
heart, has got that upside-down and has torn them away from the eyes and left   5
them standing in the heart.

    There is another mistake made by these iconoclasts, that they set about it in
disorderly fashion and not with the backing of secular authority. So their prophets
stand up and screech and egg on the mob: 'Hey, bash, rip, bite, smash, break, stab,

slash, kick, chuck, biff the idols in the mouth! When you see a crucifix, spit in its   10
face!' That is how images are abolished in Carlstadt's fashion, yea make the mob
wild and crazy and secretly accustom them to rebellion, and they then throw
themselves into the work, thinking that they are the most holy of saints, and
become so proud and brash that they are intolerable . . . For this reason we always
read in the Old Testament that where images or idols were abolished, it was not   15
the mob but the authorities who did the deed.

    Now to speak evangelically of images, I say and state that no one is obliged to
rage against God's image with the fist, but that all this is free . . . Yea, one is not
obliged to break them with the Word of God, that is, not in Carlstadt's manner
with the law, but with the Gospel, so that one instructs and enlightens the   20
conscience that it is idolatry to pray to images or to rely on them, because one
should trust in Christ alone.

    Thus, it is good and laudable that the images in Eyche, Grimmental, Birnbaum
and other places where pilgrimages are made to images (which are truly idolatrous
images and hostels of the devil) should be broken up and destroyed; but to say that   25
those who do not smash them commit sin goes too far and teaches Christians too
much.

    I have also seen and heard the iconoclasts reading my German Bible, so I know
that they possess this book and read from it, as I can tell from their words. Now
there are quite a lot of pictures in that book – of God, angels, humans and animals   30
– and especially in the Book of Revelation of St John, as well as in the books of
Moses and Joshua. So we now ask them quite amicably to allow us to do that which
they do themselves, that we might also paint pictures on the wall for the sake of
memory and better understanding, since they do as little harm on the walls as in
books. It is indeed better to depict on the walls how God created the world, how   35
Noah built the ark and whatever other good histories there are, than that one
paints some other secular and shameless scene. Indeed, would to God that I could
convince the princes and the rich to depict the whole Bible on their walls, inside
and out, for the eyes of all – that would be a Christian work.

WA, vol. 18, pp. 67, 71–5, 80

5.4   Zwingli on images, 1525

Zwingli's most extensive statement on images was written on 27 April 1525
in reply to the former territorial clerk of Uri, Valentin Compar, who
composed a number of articles and objections concerning the new beliefs
which he then had read out before the cantonal assembly at Uri. We know
of his articles only from Zwingli's reply.

Now it is said in the First Commandment, 'Thou shalt make no graven or carved
image.' Here some scholars come along, dear Valentin, just as you have noted, and
say that this prohibition is an external matter or a ceremonial triviality, and that we
Christians may have images; for the commandment only forbids making images of
God . . . One must understand that [this commandment] forbids not only the   5

likeness of the heavenly father, which some rash person has imagined for himself, but that of all gods, that is all those things which we set up as a consolation for ourselves. For if all images of gods are forbidden, then without doubt all the likenesses of those which we set up as gods are also forbidden. But what does one set up as a god? That to which each person runs with his or her concerns is a god   10
for him or her. If one has an image of this, then it is a likeness of that god and is doubly against the first commandment, first, that one has a false god and second that one has an image of it.

Now let us prove that we honour the idols in right idolatrous manner. First, we set them upon the altar before the eyes of all . . . Second, one bows and uncovers   15
one's head before them. That God has forbidden . . . Third, we lay luxury upon them with silver and gold. Now this must either happen from hope of gaining something in return, or because we seek honour from it, for otherwise one would waste their money. If it is done in hope of return, it is either because one hopes to swindle some money thereby, or else so that the idol which we decorate will give us   20
something in return, either in this life or the next. If it is done for the sake of the money, it is papal trickery . . . What we should give to the needy images of God, to the poor man, we hang on the image of man; for the idols are images of man, but man is an image of God. But if we hope to gain temporal or eternal rewards from those that are idols, it is open idolatry.   25

Fifth, we burn expensive incense before them, just as the heathens did . . . Sixth, just like the heathens, we give them the names of those they depict . . . One says 'Our Lady in Pflasterbach'. Tell me, good fellow, just who is this 'Our Lady'? Is she not wooden, just like 'Our Lady of Aachen' or 'Our Lady of Altötting'? Now if you are speaking of the mother of God, she is in heaven and not in Pflasterbach.   30
But you say: 'Surely one may tolerate images, as long as they are no longer venerated.' I say truly: No, images which have been accorded too much veneration may no more be retained than the golden calf, for they were made as a mockery of God and a diminution of his honour.

There are those who say: 'This is an image of grace' [i.e. a miraculous image],   35
and they call the idols 'holy', kissing them and behaving in similar foolish ways. And those who say, 'Our Lady in the Wannen [near Ülikon, on Lake Zurich] helped me', which words relate to no one other than to the idol which stands there. There is no difference here between the heathen idols and ours . . . For the heathens also set up their gods as being in heaven and able to do all things. The   40
devil went into them and deceived the ignorant and spoke to them through the idols, in the same way as we claim that our idols speak to us.

'The image of Christ teaches the simple, ignorant person and arouses him or her to devotion that he or she would not have without the image of Christ.' Listen to my reply, dear Valentin . . . Can anyone come to know the true lord and God   45
Jesus Christ through a dumb image without instruction in the Word? Why do we not send images to the infidels so that they may learn faith from them?

Zwingli, *Sämtliche Werke*, vol 4, pp. 91–3, 107–9, 120

5.5 Images and unchastity

A further telling criticism of religious images was that the styles of contemporary depiction were so lacking in decorum that they moved their viewers to unchaste thoughts.

5.5(a)

And even if there were no divine command against idols, they have however led to a malformed abuse which should not be tolerated. Here stands a Magdalene so whorishly painted that even the priests have always said: who can maintain devotion here and observe moderation. Yea, even the eternally pure and immaculate maid and mother of Jesus Christ had to have her breasts bared. There 5 stands a Sebastian, a Maurice and the pious John the Baptist, all so nobly, manfully and sensually [depicted] that the women had to confess because of them. And that is a disgrace, that they have to be gilded, or adorned with silver and gold or precious jewels, all of which should have been given to the poor. Yea, all makers of idols will have to account to God that they have allowed his true images to hunger 10 and suffer cold.

Zwingli, *Sämtliche Werke*, vol. 4, pp. 145–6

5.5(b)

What should one say about the great decoration in the churches, which had been brought together from gold, silver, pearls, precious jewels? And about the precious paintings in them? About the images and panels, which have cost so much? . . . In all of this, I find no trace of devotion, and cannot think that any good can come from such decoration. Indeed, when I was a youth . . . I often had bad thoughts 5 from looking upon women's images upon the altar. For no woman of pleasure would have clad or adorned herself so voluptuously or shamelessly as the mother of God, St Barbara, Katherine and others are nowadays formed.

Martin Bucer, *A Dialogue: New Karsthans* (1520)

5.6 Images and the struggle over the liturgy

The central role of images in the liturgy led to struggles between pious orthodox believers and those hostile to images. Such conflicts easily became involved with questions of status and power in parish communities, as shown in the following incident.

On the first of February 1533, Marx Ehem, churchwarden of St Moritz [in Augsburg], and two of his companions locked up the sacristy there and took the sacristy keys from the verger, and [thus] abolished the morning Masses. So the Fuggers appointed at their own expense a priest who sang early Mass daily at the high altar according to the ancient custom. Then Ehem forbade the verger to 5

set out or provide any vestments or candles for early Mass. The Fuggers put up
with this, and themselves supplied Mass vestments, a chalice, candles, lights and
an altarcloth and all that was necessary to hold early Mass. But the image of our
Lord was not laid in the Holy Sepulchre on Good Friday, because Marx Ehem
had it [the Sepulchre] sealed up . . . He also had locked up all the flags for   10
processions, incensers, monstrances, and the image of our Lord seated on a
rainbow [used] for Ascension Day, as well as images of angels and the Holy Spirit.

Now when Anthonius Fugger heard what the poisonous, godless, Zwinglian
serpent Marx Ehen had done, for the consolation and peace of the old and true
Christians he had made, secretly and at his own expense, an image of Christ on the 15
rainbow, with angels and the Holy Spirit. He paid 20 Gulden for this, so that the
usual solemn feast could be celebrated as was customary of old . . . But when Marx
Ehem got wind of this, he went to the church, and had the hole through which the
image of our Lord on the rainbow was drawn up closed off and sealed with planks,
strong timbers and iron bands. At 3 p.m. on Ascension Day the brothers Raimond   20
and Anthonius Fugger went to the church with their friends, clients and servants,
which gave great joy to the old Christians, women and men, young and old as well
as the children. For at the command of Anthonius Fugger, his foremen had gone
to the church, and used some stratagem to get the verger to open the locked doors.
Then they opened up the hole through which our Lord on the rainbow was drawn   25
up, and Ascension Day was celebrated from that hour on according to the old
custom, with great joy and reverence.

Now when Marx Ehem realised that the hole for the Ascension had been
reopened, he went hurriedly to the mayor, Ulrich Rehlinger, and told him this. He
told Ehem he should go in haste to St Moritz's, and if the Ascension had not taken 30
place, he was to command that the Rainbow was to be left standing on the floor of
the church. But if the Ascension had already taken place, he was to keep quiet, go
home and do nothing, and leave the Rainbow, the angels and all belonging to it, to
hang up above the church. Now when Ehem came into St Moritz's he had
gathered to him a bloody and tumultuous mob. There the Ascension had already   35
taken place with all reverence, according to ancient custom, and they had already
sung Nones. During the Ascension, the good old Christians cried from reverence,
and the perverted heretical Christians cursed and cried out that hellfire might
strike.

Ehem acted contrary to the mayor's command and orders, and stood in the   40
middle of the church, on the spot where the Ascension took place, and spread out
his bloody, tumultuous mob around him, as if he wanted a battle; and went up to
the verger with great abuse, and wanted to strike him for opening the church
doors. And he took the church keys from him and stood there with his unruly mob,
with half-drawn knives, and it would have required only a little for both sides to   45
attack each other: if anyone had fully drawn his knife, they would have done so . . .
Then Marx Ehem and his mob went in great anger into the choir, where the
canons and vicars were singing the Nones, and approached them with such coarse,
immodest abuse and made such a fuss that they had to stop singing, and they threw
off their surplices and fled from the church. Raimond Fugger left the church, and   50

a while later Anthonius Fugger did so as well. Then Marx Ehem and his brother Jeremiah and the unruly mob went up into the church, and let down the Rainbow and all that belonged to it. And when it was about the height of three men above the ground, Jeremiah Ehem and his companions carefully let the Rainbow fall to the ground, where it broke into pieces. Afterwards he said the rope had unintentionally slipped from their hands.

55

'Die Chronik des Clemens Sender', *Chroniken der deutschen Städte*, vol. 23, p. 342

5.7 Iconoclasm

Many of those opposed to images, such as Zwingli or Bucer, advocated orderly removal of images under the guidance of the authorities. However, evangelical zeal often led to acts of image-breaking, many of them ritual acts of punishment of failed images, of purification or even of counter-magic.

5.7(a)

1530: [25 January] Anna Mentzen from Thomerding confesses. In the recent fast days she and Anna Braitinger in play ran out of Jürgen Keller's house, where there was a spinning bee, and took the image of Christ from the Garden of Olives, and took it to Claus Keller's house, where there was also a spinning bee, and put it on a table and dragged it over before the door. Then Ulrich Keller, Marx Nibling and Hans Mair came and addressed it, and when it did not want to speak, Ulrich Keller (as he himself confessed) drew his sword and struck it, and cut off its hand. Afterwards Hans Mair carried the image into his spinning bee, and set it on the table and said: 'If you are Paul, help yourself', and thereupon knocked it from the table and sang something, I do not know what. Then they took the image and threw it from the window. Afterwards Anna Braitinger and another woman carried the image back to the Garden of Olives again.

5

10

Stadtarchiv Ulm, A5327

5.7(b)

1525: On 5 May, after we had been ejected from the Abbey [Irrsec, near Kaufbeuren], the peasants broke up the altars in the church, trod the holy relics underfoot and threw down the images from the altars, and what is much more horrible, cut the image of the infant Jesus from the arms of his mother, slit the image of St Peter down the middle, sprinkled it with baptismal water, turned it upside down and tore out its insides.

5

P. Marcus Furter, *Historia belli rusticorum*, 1525

5.7(c)

1524: On Easter Monday [28 March] at six in the morning [the mob] broke into the Franciscan church, then through the barriers and the door to the choir, and they took out the image of St Francis and set it in the stocks, and then, so the people say, they cut off its head.

'Regesten der Stadt Königsberg', *Altpreussische Monatsschrift*, 18 (1881), p. 38

5.8   Images and evangelical piety

Despite the hostility of Zwingli and the radicals to images, they continued to play an important role in evangelical piety. In Brandenburg, where the Elector believed that the use of images served a pedagogic function, many of the popular Catholic elements in the liturgy were retained, including the use of images, as the statutes of 1540 show.

On the feast of the Ascension, the spectacle with the ascension of the lord shall remain, where it is in use, for such spectacles serve as a good remembrance for youth and the simple. The same on the feast of Pentecost, with the lowering of the holy spirit, but the pouring of water and all other abuses of the same kind shall be omitted. The preachers shall always instruct the young about what these ceremonies signify, for otherwise they would be useless, and especially indicate that one does not thereby become pious or justified before God, or through such external things, but that this occurs only through faith in Jesus Christ alone.

Sehling, *Die evangelischen Kirchenordnungen des xvi. Jhts*, vol. 3, p. 88

Questions

1   List the different reasons for the condemnation of images in worship.
2   How did Luther's views differ from those of Carlstadt and Zwingli?
3   Why did some evangelical believers approve of the use of images?
4   What non-religious issues were involved in disagreements over images?
5   Why did the removal of images so often become disorderly?
6   Why could it be said that the destroyers of images were as enslaved to them as their supporters?

II: The conflict over the Eucharist

The Eucharist was central to pre-Reformation religious belief, not least because of the claim that Christ was truly present in the consecrated elements of bread and wine. It is not surprising that it should have constituted a major focus of attention for religious reformers. The complexity of the doctrine and its manifestations in popular belief ensured that there would also be disagreement about it among evangelical believers. The lines of debate were quickly apparent and revolved around the same issues that had agitated the late-medieval church: in what way the presence of Christ in the elements was to be understood, whether as a real or as a symbolic presence. This debate had considerable implications for liturgical practice as well as for popular belief, not least the dangers, in the eyes of theologians, of popular misunderstanding and consequent religious or secular disorder.

5.9 Luther's reply to the Christians in Reutlingen, 4 January 1526

Zwingli had formulated his position on the Eucharist at an early stage, although he did not push it too quickly into prominence. However, in order to win support for his interpretation, he did write to Mattheus Alber, the preacher in the imperial city of Reutlingen, in the hope of winning the community there to his side. Alber turned to Luther for his view of the matter, provoking the following 'pastoral letter' in which Luther sought decisively to turn the Reutlingers away from the 'sacramentarian' position.

You are no doubt aware that our enemy the devil has beset us and rages and roars like an angry lion, and seeks how he might devour us . . . Therefore he has attacked us with sects, hordes, heretics and false spirits, especially over the holy Sacrament of baptism and the Sacrament of the altar . . . I mean those who teach that in the Sacrament of the altar is mere bread and wine, but not the true body 5 and blood of Christ . . . These sects have three heads, for although they agree that there is mere bread and wine in the Sacrament, they disagree about why and on what grounds that is so.
   The first head and spirit [Carlstadt] gives this reason, that the words 'Do this [in memory of me]' indicate Christ seated [at the Last Supper] and not the bread, and 10 you know that Dr Carlstadt gives this reason, and I have written against it. This is rejected by the other head or spirit, which gives another reason, namely that the little word 'is' means 'signifies' or 'symbolises', as Zwingli or Oecolampadius jest in torturing and making a fool of Scripture and its words . . . However, the third head or spirit [Caspar Schwenckfeld] rejects this, and will have neither 'do this' 15 nor 'signifies', but twists the words and makes of them the following: 'My body is given for you as a spiritual food' . . . See how the puffed-up fleshly meaning twists and turns and seeks a way not to remain by God's Word. What sort of spirit is this, that is so unsure of itself in a single matter and so in disagreement that each of these three heads swears it is right and damns the others. I do not call such things 20 subtle but a coarse and palpable devil, which God has allowed, for our good, to bite, tear and eat one another up, so that this disunited kingdom will be destroyed by itself and not lead us astray.

So I beseech you, my beloved ones, to stick to the simple and direct words of
Christ with which he bestowed the Sacrament of his body and blood, saying: 'Take   25
and eat, this is my body, which has been given for you', etc. They may write and
gloss it as they like, the text is there, the words are plain and clear, and they will not
be able to make something else out of them with any reasonable basis . . . If the
reason given by the first spirit, Dr Carlstadt, which had more substance to it than
the others, is invalid, then the others are even more so.   30

WA, vol. 19, pp. 119–25 *passim*

5.10   Zwingli's awareness of the seriousness of the dispute, 1525

I had held these views of the Eucharist for several years, but it was my plan not to
scatter them thoughtlessly among the common people, so that I did not cast pearls
before swine, without having first discussed them frequently with learned and
pious men. Thus, this most important matter of all, as all agree, would have many
defenders when it was presented publicly, and avoid the kind of noisy envy which   5
solely through senseless cries of rage would have deterred pious minds from
reading, listening and judging it. My plan progressed as I desired.

Cited in *WA*, vol. 19, p. 114

5.11   The problem of irreverence

Disagreement about the nature of the Eucharist possibly led to increasing
popular scepticism about the Sacrament and irreverence towards it. There
were many open acts of profanity, which confirmed the worst fears of
conservative evangelical thinkers that continual disagreement on the
subject could only lead to unrest. Events during the Peasants' War, in
which the elements of the Sacrament were regularly profaned, confirmed
these fears.

5.11(a)   *A parody of the Mass, 1525*

In the peasants' rebellion Blesi Krieg, along with others, entered the convent at
Oberried, therein smashed the pyx containing the Host with a blacksmith's
hammer; carried the Host to the altar in a monstrance, which he then also
smashed; thereafter took the Host from the monstrance and laid it on the altar;
apart from it there were five particles [of the Host] on a paten in a bag, which he   5
took up to the altar and tipped out of the bag. Hans, Schilt's cowherd, Seger's
maid, Michel Riegk's cowherd, these four, and he took the five particles, stuffed
them in each other's mouths, he [Krieg] eating his. Thereupon he donned priest's
robes, sang Mass, elevated the Host which he had removed from the monstrance
in mockery and contempt, displayed it to the others, who had to ring the Sanctus   10
bells, and set it down again. Then he consumed the Host in the manner of a priest.

Scott and Scribner, p. 108 (no.20)

5.11(b)   *Irreverence towards the Sacrament in Augsburg, 1528*

1528, on Good Friday (10 April) as the most venerable Sacrament was laid in a
tabernacle in the holy Sepulchre in St Ulrich's, according to ancient custom, a
man went up to it and said: 'Shame on you, Christ, what are you doing in that
fool's cage?', and then in mockery bared his bottom at it. After Easter the
venerable Sacrament was stolen from the altar in which it was reserved in St   5
Anna's church. The town council offered a reward of 100 florins for information
about the thief, but it was held to be a prank and nothing further was done about it.
It was rumoured that renegade monks had done it themselves.

'Die Chronik des Clemens Sender', p. 197

5.12   The Marburg Colloquy – divergent interpretations

The Marburg Colloquy, sponsored by Margrave Philip of Hesse and held
on 2–4 October 1529 was an attempt to resolve the different views of
Luther and Zwingli on the Eucharist. An ambiguous formula was agreed,
allowing each side to uphold its own interpretation and feel it had been
vindicated.

5.12(a)   *Luther to his wife Katherina, 4 October 1529*

Know that our amicable conference at Marburg is now at an end and that we are
almost in agreement on all points except that our opponents maintain that there is
mere bread and wine in the Lord's Supper, and that Christ is only present in a
spiritual sense. Today the landgrave intervened to bring us to agreement, hoping
that although we disagreed we would still regard each other as brothers and   5
members of Christ. He tried hard, but we would not call them brothers or
members of Christ although we wish them well and desire to remain at peace . . .
Tell Bugenhagen that Zwingli's best argument was that a body could not exist
without occupying space and therefore Christ's body was not in the bread, and that
Oecolampadius' best argument was that the Sacrament is only the sign of Christ's   10
body. I think God blinded them so that they could not get beyond these points.

WA **Briefwechsel, vol. 4, p. 154**

5.12(b)   *Zwingli to Vadian, 20 October 1529*

I'll give you a brief account of what you are so anxious to learn . . . Luther,
Melanchthon, Oecolampadius and Zwingli entered the arena in the presence of
the landgrave and a few others, twenty-four at most. We fought it out . . . before
witnesses to a winning battle over four sessions in all. Three times we threw at
Luther the fact that he had at other times given a different exposition from the one 5
he was now upholding, those ludicrous ideas of his that Christ suffered in his
divine nature, that the body of Christ is everywhere, and that the flesh profits
nothing. But that fine fellow had nothing at all to say in reply, except that on

the matter of the flesh profiting nothing he said: 'You know, Zwingli, that all the
ancient writers have time and again changed their interpretation of passages   10
of Scripture as time went on and their judgement matured.' He said: 'The body of
Christ is eaten and received into our body in the bodily sense, but at the same time
I reserve my judgement on whether the human spirit eats his body too.' But a little
before he had said: 'The body of Christ is eaten by the mouth in the bodily sense,
but the human spirit does not eat him in the bodily sense.' He said: 'The body of   15
Christ is constituted by saying the words "This is my body", however great a
criminal the person saying them might be.' He conceded that the body of Christ is
finite. He conceded that the Eucharist might be called a sign of the body of Christ.

These are examples of the countless inconsistencies, the absurdities and
stupidities which he bleats out like a babbling brook. But we refuted him so   20
successfully that the landgrave himself now agrees with us, although he conceals it
before the other princes. The Hessian party has almost all abandoned Luther's
position. The landgrave himself has given permission for our books to be read with
impunity and in future will not allow bishops who share our views to be removed
from office.   25

We left Marburg with certain agreements which you will soon see in writing.
The truth prevailed so manifestly that if ever a man was beaten it was Luther – for
all his impudence and obstinacy – and everyone witnessed it too, although of
course the judge was discreet and impartial. Even so, Luther kept protesting that
he had not been beaten. However, we have achieved this much good, that our   30
agreement on the rest of the doctrines of the Christian religion will preclude the
papal party from hoping any longer that Luther will come over to them.

Zwingli, *Sämtliche Werke*, vol. 10, pp. 316–18

5.13   The impact on liturgical practice

The Zwinglian communion service in Zurich was refashioned to give
expression to the doctrine that the elements remained merely bread and
wine and that any transformation was symbolic. In Lutheran areas, the
desire to avoid any implication of a Zwinglian reading of the Eucharist, as
well as the Lutheran concern for weak consciences, led to considerable
conservatism in liturgical practice, with the preservation of numerous
aspects of the papal Mass: the retention of a predominantly Latin service,
celebrated by a priest in traditional vestments, the use of the wafer in the
celebration of communion and the retention of the Elevation, accompanied
by the ringing of bells to indicate the completed consecration. Some
outside observers found it difficult to distinguish such a service from the
Mass.

5.13(a)   *The communion service in Zurich, 1525*

After this the appointed ministers carry around the unleavened bread, and each believer takes with his own hand a piece or mouthful from it, or has it given him by the minister who carried the bread around. And when those with the bread have gone around and each has eaten his small piece the other ministers likewise follow behind them with the wine and similarly give each person some of it to drink. And all this is done with such reverence and decorum as is entirely suitable for such a godly community and the Lord's Supper.

Zwingli, *Sämtliche Werke*, vol. 4, p. 23

5.13(b)   *The celebration of Lutheran Mass in Eisenach, 1536*

The following account was written by Wolfgang Musculus, pastor of the Holy Cross Church in Augsburg, after attending a Lutheran service in Eisenach on 14 May 1536. The Zwinglian tendencies in Augsburg clearly influenced the note of disapproval in the report.

At 7 a.m. we entered the church where the office of the so-called Mass was celebrated in the following fashion. First, the Introit 'Cantate Domino' was sung in Latin by the schoolboys and their teacher, standing apart in the choir, wholly in the papist manner. This was followed by the Kyrie Eleison, during which the organ was played. Third, a celebrant clad [in Mass vestments] according to papist custom stood before the altar decorated in equally papist style with candles and other things and sang in Latin 'Gloria in excelsis Deo'. The choir continued this hymn to its end, alternating with the organ. When the Gloria was finished the celebrant sang a so-called Collect in German, facing the altar and with his back to the people. Then, turning to the people he added a reading in German from the Epistle of St James. Then the organ was played again and the choir sang 'Victimae paschali' . . . In between they sang in German: 'Christ is risen'. The celebrant now sang the Gospel in German, facing the people. After this reading, the organ played and the entire church sang in German 'We all believe in one God'. When all this was finished, Justus Menius preached, without any vestments and clad only in street clothes.

When the sermon was finished the celebrant, dressed like a priest, admonished the congregation to pray for certain needs, which were listed in detail, concluding with Christ's injunction that 'whatever you ask the Father in my name, etc.'. Then he held a brief admonition on the institution of the Lord's Supper and then sang the words [of consecration] for the Supper, first the words for the bread, whereupon he elevated the bread entirely in the papist fashion while the people sank to their knees, then the words for the chalice, which was also elevated after saying Christ's words. After that had been done the organ was played, alternating with the choir singing the 'Agnus Dei', during which communion was distributed, whereby the chalice was offered by a clergyman in secular clothes. However, not a single man came forward to take communion, only a couple of female communicants. After they had communicated, the celebrant communicated himself, after genuflecting before the bread; this he did not do before the chalice, merely drinking it out carefully, then pouring in more wine with which to cleanse   30 the chalice, so that none of the Blood [of Christ] remained. After the communion, he sang a prayer with his face to the altar, after which he dismissed the people with a sung blessing. Finally, as the people left the church, the choir sang in German 'Grant us thy peace' and the celebration was thus finished.

T. Kolde, *Analecta Lutherana*, Gotha, 1883, pp. 216–17

5.14   The Elevation encourages the survival of traditional belief

The continued use of the Elevation, retained in Electoral Saxony until 1543, encouraged many to persist in traditional popular beliefs, something which caused great concern to Philip Melanchthon. However, the practice was not so easily eradicated, especially where it was popular among both clergy and parishioners. Ducal Saxony, first reformed in 1539, experienced the same difficulties as Electoral Saxony.

5.14(a)   *Daniel Gretser's complaints, 1543*

[Because of the retention of the Elevation] many come neither to the sermon, nor to the Psalms nor to other prayers held in the church during divine service. Rather they stand outside chattering and whatever, but as soon as they hear the bells [accompanying the Elevation], they peep into the church, hold up their hands in prayer, kiss them afterwards and go away, thinking that they have received a great   5 part of the Sacrament in as far as they have only gazed upon it.

L. Fendt, *Der lutherische Gottesdienst des 16. Jahrhunderts*, Munich, 1923, p. 189

5.14(b)   *Melanchthon to Andreas Lauterbach, 1 April 1543*

I am sending you Friedrich Myconius's letter, from which you will learn that the Elevation has been abolished by the synod in many places [in Thuringia]. For the Elevation confirms two pernicious errors, transsubstantiation and the error that the Mass is a sacrifice. How great a false adoration has grown out of this error will be revealed in the Last Days, when Christ will lay bare the sins of the world.   5

Corpus Reformatorum, vol. 5, p. 82

5.15   The persistence of the Elevation

Popular insistence on the retention of the Elevation, despite official attempts to abolish it, led to lack of uniformity in Lutheran practice.

5.15(a)   *Church statutes for Celle in ducal Saxony, 1545*

Memorandum on the Elevation: where the Elevation has been abolished, it shall so
remain for a while, but where it is still in use, it shall be tolerated for a while.
Thereby one must consider that it is more useful and better serves improvement,
and conforms more to Christ's institution [of the Sacrament] that the priest turns
around from the altar and consecrates facing the people . . . also that he should not   5
sing the words of consecration, but say them aloud clearly, and consecrate the
Sacrament facing the church, as stated. But this is not to be done without first
consulting our gracious prince Duke Moritz of Saxony and hearing his princely
grace's gracious opinion and decision. But if one is minded to commence this
practice, the people should be instructed beforehand, so that it might begin   10
without trouble.

Sehling, *Die evangelischen Kirchenordnungen des xvi. Jhts*, vol. 1/i, p. 301

5.15(b)   *Church statutes for the principality of Anhalt, 1568*

Since the Elevation of the most worthy Sacrament of the true body and blood of
Christ is accepted in some churches but not in others, the clergy are ordered to
elevate it on solemn feasts, but otherwise the most estimable prince Bernhard is
content that it should be omitted. Similarly, the surplice is to be used for all three
Sunday sermons, but during the week it may not be used.   5

Sehling, *Die evangelischen Kirchenordnungen des xvi. Jhts*, vol. 1/ii, p. 570

Questions

1   How does Luther's letter in **5.9** clarify the different views of the
Eucharist held by Zwingli and himself?

2   In **5.9** and **5.10** it is clear that Zwingli has not made an issue of his
views about the Eucharist. Why did he prefer to keep a low-key
position about this?

3   How do the incidents related in **5.11** link to those in **5.7**? Are the
motives comparable?

4   (a) What was the main issue under discussion at Marburg?
(b) Why was Philip of Hesse so anxious to bring about agreement on
this matter?
(c) Which side of the argument seems clearer and more acceptable?
(d) What feelings did Luther and Zwingli have about each other?
(e) What political outcome did Zwingli foresee?

5   Using two parallel columns, show what were the main differences
between the Zwinglian and the Lutheran celebrations of communion as
described in **5.13(a)** and **5.13(b)**.

6   What is meant by the 'Elevation'? Why was this considered an abuse? Why was it so difficult to eradicate as a practice? What was the link between this and the debate about images?

7   How has your overall understanding of the Protestant Reformation been helped by this more detailed study of two central and practical concerns of the Reformers?

6 The religious radicals

Documents in earlier chapters have revealed how far religious and other developments diverged from those ideas of Luther which precipitated the reform movements. It did not take long for more radical tendencies to emerge. Some were like the Zwickau prophets, whose radical ideas pre-dated Luther, but who were given a more serious hearing because of the intense religious excitement generated by the initial upsurge of reform. Others were the 'false brethren', those like Carlstadt or the Swiss Anabaptists who drew more radical conclusions from the ideas of Luther and Zwingli than the two leading reformers of the 1520s were willing to accept. A third stream was influenced by the new evangelical theology, but blended it with pre-Reformation mystical and apocalyptical ideas. These included figures such as Thomas Müntzer or Melchior Hoffman, who forged their own distinctive understanding of the Gospel and what it demanded. Reformers such as Luther or Zwingli viewed these developments as dangerous and a threat to their own work of reform, especially when such ideas took the form of direct action or a direct challenge to traditional Christian ideas about secular authority, the nature of the believing community or such a fundamental issue as baptism. Radical religious thought was a coat of many colours. After the upheavals of the Peasants' War and the involvement of some radicals in insurrectionary millennialist movements, secular authorities tended to tar all radicals with the same brush, however inaccurate the labels. A few authorities took a tolerant view, most notably the city of Strassburg, which at first allowed radicals to live peacefully in its midst so long as they did not attempt to propagate their views. Many radical groups, however, followed the path of the Hutterites, and sought to establish their own communities in areas remote from the main centres of Reformation activity.

6.1 The Zwickau prophets in Wittenberg, 1522

The early arrival of visionary prophets in Wittenberg was the first sign of the future disruption of evangelical unity.

Ambrosius Wilcken, news from Wittenberg

A new prophet [Marcus Stübner, one of the so-called Zwickau prophets] was here some days ago. I did not see him, but it is said that he has many revelations from God, who had spoken to him often. He was formerly in Prague in Bohemia and preached there, but they did not wish to hear him and stoned him. Philip   5 Melanchthon has spoken to him often at home, so [much so] that he does not know what to do with him . . . Other Doctors gave him a hearing and asked him many things, such as what he preached and who bade him to preach it. To the latter he replied: 'Our Lord God'. Asked whether he had written books, he replied: 'No, our Lord God had forbidden it.' Now Philip was quite disconcerted   10 by him, and forbade the students to worry him. Someone has written to the Elector to send Martin here, [because Stübner] referred to him, saying that he must come to him. He also said that Martin was right most times, but not on all points, and that someone higher than him would come with a superior spirit. Item, [he said that]: the Turk would invade Germany; that the priests would all be slain unless   15 they took wives; that very soon, in five, six or seven years there would be such alterations in the world that no impious or wicked sinner would be left alive; then there would be one entrance, one baptism, one faith; the children who are baptised before they reach the age of reason have no baptism. Thus, many learned persons say that he has a spirit, whether it be good or evil.   20

Müller, *Wittenberg Bewegung* **pp. 415–16 (no. 68)**

Questions

1   Why was Marcus Stübner called a 'prophet'?
2   On what points did he disagree with Luther?
3   Why was Philip Melanchthon so impressed by him?

6.2   Luther and the 'false brethren'

Luther's concern about those evangelical preachers with whom he disagreed radically over various points of doctrine and procedures of reform led him to stigmatise them as 'fanatics' and 'mob spirits'. The activities of Carlstadt, Müntzer and others also aroused the concern of princes afraid of disturbance. After a personal encounter with Carlstadt in which Luther effectively threw down the gauntlet, he went to Orlamunde, where Carlstadt had been elected preacher, in order to warn the community against him. However, Luther's personal attempts to intervene in favour of his ideas of reform did not always meet with a positive response. Such encounters led Luther to rethink his position on some basic issues of reform: whether communities had an unqualified right to elect their own pastors, whether the lay person could interpret the Word as effectively as the scholar, and how far reform was possible without the sheltering hand of princely authority. His decisions on these matters were to move the Lutheran variety of reform decisively away from its early popular emphasis.

Luther confronts Carlstadt and the community of Orlamunde, 24 August 1524
The mayor thanked Luther on behalf of the council and entire community for showing such resolution and coming to them in response to their letter, and they begged him for God's sake that he would preach to them. But Dr Martin replied that he had not come to preach to them, but that he had their letter and wanted to discuss it with the council and commune . . . He took the letter from the town of   5
Orlamunde in his hand and asked if the council recognised the seal as their own. The council and commune replied that they did. Dr Martin said: 'I regard you as simple folk, and I do not think it credible that you could have written this letter . . . I fear that Carlstadt wrote the letter and sent it under the city seal.' Whereupon the council and commune replied that Carlstadt had written no single syllable of the   10
letter, nor had he used the city seal. Then Dr Martin read the letter out from beginning to end . . . Afterwards Dr Martin spoke about certain articles, and especially where he had read: 'Our parish priest and pastor Andreas Carlstadt said . . .'. Luther said: 'You call him your pastor, but my lord the Elector Frederick and the University of Wittenberg know nothing of this, and he will not be   15
accepted.' Whereupon a city treasurer replied: 'If Carlstadt is not our pastor, then Paul had taught falsely and your books must also be false, for we have elected him, as our letter to the University shows and contains'.
     The city secretary said to Martin Luther: 'You have written, as can be proved from your own writings, that you have included us Orlamunders among the   20
fanatics and giddy spirits, and regarded us as if we act and behave like those in Allstedt, because we have abolished images and freely confess this . . . Then Luther said: 'How will you prove from Scripture that images should be abolished?' A member of the town council spoke up: 'My lord doctor, amiable brother, you must admit that Moses is an expounder of the Ten Commandments?' Martin said;   25
'Yes.' The councillor went on: 'It is written in the Ten Commandments "Thou shalt have no strange gods", and directly afterwards Moses goes on to explain "Thou shalt remove all images and have none".' Martin said: 'Yes, that is said of idolatrous images. Idolatrous images are those to which one prays. How does a crucifix on the wall harm me if I do not pray to it?' A cobbler said: 'I have often   30
taken my hat off to an image on the wall or on the street. This is idolatry, dishonour to God and harmful to poor folk, and therefore one should have no images.' Martin said: 'If you [do this] because of misuse, you would have to slay all women and pour away all wine.' Another member of the commune replied: 'No, they are God's creatures, created for our help, sustenance and need, and which he   35
has not commanded us to be rid of. But the images made by the hand of man we are commanded to abolish.' Dr Martin however insisted on the words 'idolatrous images'. The cobbler went on: 'Yes, I would concede this if all images were not forbidden by Moses.' Martin Luther said: 'That is not in holy Scripture.' The cobbler said: 'Say what you will, it is there', and he clapped his hands together and   40
made a bet . . . Someone brought in the books of Moses and the text was read out to Martin [Deut. 5: 15–17].

'From this it plainly follows that not only the idolatrous, but all images are forbidden, indeed that Christians may make and have no images.' To which Martin said: 'It is there written that you should pray to no images, and God   45
therefore meant the idolatrous.' Then someone from the commune said: 'The word "idolatrous" is not in the text, but only "thou shalt make and have none" . . .
Then Martin said: 'He is again speaking of "idolatrous images".'

The mayor then spoke: 'Listen, good lord, listen.' There was a great silence and he went on: 'Dear lord, we keep strictly to the Word of God, for it is written that   50
you should add nothing to it or take nothing away.' Then the prince's preacher spoke out: 'Be quiet, my dear old man.' Martin went on: 'You have condemned me.' The cobbler replied: 'If you want to be condemned, I hold you as condemned along with whoever speaks or reads against God and God's truth.' Martin said: 'The children on the streets have said that to me!' and he stood up and began to   55
hurry towards his wagon. As the city treasurer saw that, he said: 'Hey, dear doctor, tell us about the articles on the Sacrament and Baptism.' To which Martin turned around and said: 'I have written enough about this, read my books.' His challenger replied: 'I have read parts of them, but I do not find that my conscience is thereby satisfied.' To which Martin replied: 'If you stumble over it, then write against me.'   60

WA, vol. 15, pp. 322–47 *passim*

Questions

1 Why did Luther visit Orlamunde?
2 What were the main points at issue between him and the citizens there?
3 Why did Luther think the citizens of Orlamunde were 'fanatics and giddy spirits' [line 21]?
4 How does this encounter suggest that Luther has changed some of his ideas?

6.3 The debate with the Anabaptists in Zurich, 17 January 1525

Two aspects of Zwingli's teaching in Zurich led to the emergence of the more radical brand of evangelical believers usually called 'Anabaptists'. The first was his insistence on the Bible as the sole guide for Christian life; the second was his initial reservation about the validity of infant baptism. Adopting a strict literalism in their interpretation of the Bible, and following the argument that most of the traditional Sacraments were not to be found there, they extended this to infant baptism. This was linked to the idea that being a Christian should be a voluntary choice, made in faith, by those old enough to make a right choice. Although these ideas were abroad in Zurich from 1523, the Anabaptists first became an issue in 1525, when the implications of their beliefs began to trouble both Zwingli and the secular authorities.

A disputation was arranged by the magistrates on 17 January at the town hall before the town council, the citizens of Zurich and the scholars. The aforesaid persons, especially Mantz, Grebel, Roubli, stood up and presented the reasons why children could not believe and did not understand what baptism was. Baptism should be given to those believers to whom the Gospel had already been preached, 5 who understood it and themselves requested baptism and who wanted to slay the old Adam and live a new life. Children knew nothing at all about this, so baptism was not appropriate for them. They pointed out passages from the Gospels and the Acts of the Apostles showing that the Apostles had not baptised children but only adults who understood it. One should do exactly as the Apostles did. Since 10 baptism has hitherto not been practised in this way, the baptism of children was invalid and each person should be rebaptised.

Zwingli replied methodically, in the same way as is set out in his 'Grounds and Reply', a book he had written to those of St Gallen about infant baptism and rebaptism. The Baptists could neither refute his arguments nor credibly sustain 15 their views . . . When the disputation was finished, the Baptists were earnestly warned by the authorities to desist and to be quiet, since they were not able to uphold their cause with God's Word. That had no effect on them, for they said that they must obey God rather than men, and so the unrest and division became greater the longer it went on. 20

On 20 March . . . the town council spoke very seriously to them and admonished them to desist, since their scandalous separation and division would not longer be tolerated. Some were kept in prison but others were expelled from the land, but that achieved nothing other than that they persisted in their ways . . .

As said above, Anabaptism increased considerably in the city and territory of 25 Zurich . . . Grebel, Mantz and other prominent Baptists had gathered so many folk around them that many people in this lordship had become disobedient and seditious.

Bullinger, *Reformationsgeschichte*, vol. 1, pp. 238–9, 294–5

Questions

1 Why did the Anabaptists reject infant baptism?
2 Why were they accused of being seditious?
3 What does this episode tell us about the Swiss Anabaptists' relationship with the authorities?

6.4   Thomas Müntzer and millennialist religion

Thomas Müntzer, Luther's other major opponent within evangelical ranks alongside Carlstadt, combined a mystical, spiritualist approach to faith with a radical activist streak, which turned him into a genuinely revolutionary thinker. Believing – as did many of his contemporaries, Luther included – that the Last Days were at hand, he called for decisive intervention to end the suffering of the Christian people, a suffering he interpreted as both social and spiritual. In 1524 he still had hopes that godly princes would undertake this task, shown in his sermon before the Saxon princes and future Electors, Duke John of Saxony and his son John Frederick, delivered in Allstedt on 13 July 1524. The sermon expounded the Second Chapter of the Book of Daniel, a classic millennialist text, although Müntzer drew from it characteristic conclusions which clearly distinguished him from both Lutherans and other millennialists.

The Sermon to the Princes, 13 July 1524
It is true – I know it for a fact – that the spirit of God is revealing to many elect and pious men at this time the great need for a full and final reformation in the near future. This must be carried out. For despite all attempts to oppose it the prophecy of Daniel remains in full force – whether anyone believes it or not, as Paul says in Romans 3. This text of Daniel, then, is as clear as the bright sun, and the work of ending the fifth Empire of the world is now in full swing. The first Empire is explained by the golden knob – that was the Babylonian – the second by the silver breastplate and arm-piece – that was the Empire of the Medes and Persians. The third was the Greek Empire, resonant with human cleverness, indicated by the bronze; the fourth the Roman Empire, an empire won by the sword, an empire ruled by force. But the fifth is the one we see before us, which is also of iron and would like to use force, but is patched with dung. 5

Therefore, my dearest, most revered rulers, learn true judgement from the mouth of God himself . . . I know this for a fact, that if the plight of the Christian people really came home to you and you put your mind to it properly then you would develop the same zeal as King Jehu showed, 2 Kings 9, 10, and as we find throughout the whole book of Revelation. And I know this for a fact that you would have the very greatest difficulty not to resort to the power of the sword. For the condition of the holy people of Christ has become so pitiable, that up to now not even the most eloquent tongue could do it justice. Therefore a new Daniel must arise and expound your dreams to you . . . For once you really grasp the plight of the Christian people as a result of the treachery of the false clergy and the abandoned criminals, your rage against them will be boundless, beyond all imagining . . . For they have made such a fool of you that everyone swears . . . that princes are just pagans, that all they have to do is to maintain civic order. 10 15 20 25

Now if you are to be true rulers, you must seize the very roots of government, following the command of Christ. Drive his enemies away from the elect; you are the instrument to do this. My friend, don't let us have any of these hackneyed posturings about the power of God achieving everything without any resort to your sword; otherwise it may rust in its scabbard . . . Our scholars come and – in their godless and fraudulent way – understand Daniel to say that the Antichrist should be destroyed without human hands . . . To ensure, however, that this proceeds in a fair and orderly manner, our revered fathers the princes, who with us confess Christ, should carry it out. But if they do not carry it out the sword will be taken from them, Daniel 7:27. 30 35

P. Matheson (ed.), *The Collected Works of Thomas Müntzer*, Edinburgh, 1988, pp. 244–5, 246, 250

6.5   Müntzer as revolutionary, 1525

Müntzer's appeal to the princes fell on deaf ears, so that he turned to the people to carry out the task of punishing the godless. When he was attempting to raise a revolutionary army to carry out his vision in 1525, he turned for support to his old congregation in Allstedt. Written at the height of success of the peasant rebellion, the letter breathes the militant spirit that made Müntzer so feared by the authorities.

Open Letter to the People of Allstedt, 26/7 April 1525
May the pure fear of God be with you, dear brothers. How long are you going to slumber, how long are you going to resist God's will . . . ? If you are unwilling to suffer for the sake of God, then you will have to be martyrs for the devil . . . The whole of Germany, France, Italy is awake; the master wants to set the game in   5
motion, the evil-doers are for it. At Fulda four abbeys were laid waste during Easter week, the peasants in the Klettgau and the Hegau in the Black Forest have risen, three thousand strong.
     Even if there are only three of you whose trust in God is imperturbable and who seek his name and honor alone, you need have no fear of a hundred thousand. So   10
go to it, go to it, go to it! The time has come, the evil-doers are running like scared dogs! . . . Pay no attention to the cries of the godless . . . they will whimper and wheedle like children. Show no pity, as God has commanded in the words of Moses, Deuteronomy 7: [1–5] . . . Alert the villages and towns and especially the mineworkers and other good fellows who will be of use. We cannot slumber any   15
longer.
     Go to it, go to it, while the fire is hot. Hammer away ding-dong on the anvils of Nimrod [i.e. the princes and lords], cast down their tower to the ground! As long as they live it is impossible for you to rid yourselves of the fear of men . . . Go to it, go to it, while it is day. God goes before you; follow, follow . . . This is what God   20
says, 'You should have no fear. You should not shrink from this great host; it is not your fight, but the Lord's'.
Mühlhausen, in the year 1525.
Thomas Müntzer, a servant of God against the godless.

Matheson, pp. 140–2

Questions

1   What is meant by 'millennialist' and 'millenarian'?
2   In **6.4**, how does Müntzer try to persuade the princes to act against the clergy and the papal church? What course of action does he suggest?
3   What does **6.4** tell us about Müntzer and his beliefs?
4   Why did Müntzer believe revolutionary action was necessary?
5   How is **6.5** different from **6.4**, and why?

Johann Liechtenbergers.
Dieser Prophet sihet dem Thomas Müntzer gleich

Das xxix. Capitel.

WAnn sich nun vil Secten vnnd Rotten erheben/
vnd die leut sich auff vil newe ding in kurtzen Jaren vnder disen jetzerzeltenzeitten befleissen wer
den/da wirt sich ein klüger/weiser/wolberedter man her
fürmachen. wann er zu den Jaren der vernunfft kompt

Thomas Müntzer as False Prophet, in Johann Lichtenberger, *Propheceien und Weissagungen*.
Lutheran propaganda against Thomas Müntzer led to him being stigmatised as a false prophet. There are no contemporary portraits of Müntzer, but his reputation suggested that his name could be inscribed over the depiction of any false prophet, as was done here with the inscription placed over this illustration of a scholar preaching outdoors to attentive lay people: 'This prophet looks like Thomas Müntzer'.

6.6   Conrad Grebel to Thomas Müntzer, 5 September 1524

The Swiss Anabaptists recognised in Müntzer someone who shared their views on faith and infant baptism, and who dared to criticise the shortcomings of other evangelical preachers, and Grebel wrote to establish contact. However, they diverged from him on the important matter of the sword.

Dear brother Thomas . . . Our forefathers fell away from the true God and knowledge of Jesus Christ, from the one, true, common divine Word, from divine practices, and from Christian life and love, and lived without God's law and gospel in useless human and unchristian customs and ceremonies, believing that they would attain salvation thereby and yet falling short of it, as the evangelical   5
preachers have shown . . . In the same way, everyone today wants to be saved by superficial faith, without the fruits of faith, without the baptism of trial and probation, without love and hope, without right Christian practices, and wants to persist . . . in the common ritualistic and antichristian customs of baptism and the Lord's Supper, in contempt of the divine Word and out of respect for the word of   10
the pope and of the anti-papal preachers.

   We also fell into the same error as long as we heard and read only the evangelical preachers who are to blame for all this, as a punishment for our sins. But after we also took Scripture in hand and consulted it on many points, we have become rather better informed and have discovered the great and harmful error of   15
the shepherds.

   While we were noting and deploring these facts, your book against false faith and baptism reached us, and we were more fully instructed and confirmed, and it rejoiced us wonderfully to have found someone of like Christian mind, and who dared to show the evangelical preachers their failings.   20

   However, the Gospel and its adherents are not to be protected by the sword . . . which we learn from our brother is your opinion and practice. True Christian believers are sheep among wolves, sheep for the slaughter; they must be baptised in anguish and affliction, tribulation, persecution, suffering and death; they must be tried with fire and must reach the fatherland of eternal rest not by slaying their   25
fleshly enemies but by mortifying them spiritually. They use neither the worldly sword nor war, since all killing has ceased with them – unless we would indeed still be under the old law.

Thomas Müntzer, *Schriften und Briefe*, edited by G. Franz, Gütersloh, 1968, pp. 438–9, 442

6.7   The Schleitheim Confession, 1527

By 1527 the radical wing of the evangelical movement had grown rapidly, and encompassed great diversity of belief, although the main doctrine uniting its many small groups seems to be repudiation of infant baptism. A meeting was arranged of some of the main groups of south German and Swiss Anabaptists in Schleitheim, a small town on the Swiss–German border, and a common basis of belief was drawn up by Michael Sattler. Anabaptism remained a heterogeneous movement and not all groups agreed with many of the propositions in the Schleitheim Confession. However, it remains the best summary of the major tenets of Anabaptism and explains why secular authorities were often so hostile to this version of Reformation belief.

The articles which we discussed and on which we were of one mind are: (1) Baptism; (2) the Ban; (3) Breaking of Bread; (4) Separation from the Abomination; (5) Pastors in the Church; (6) the Sword; and (7) the Oath.

(4) We are agreed as follows on separation. A separation shall be made from the evil and wickedness which the devil planted in the world; in this manner, simply   5
that we shall have no fellowship with the wicked and not run with them in the multitude of their abominations . . . From all this we should learn that everything which is not united with our God and Christ cannot be other than an abomination which we should shun and flee from. By this is meant all popish and anti-popish works and church services, meetings and church attendance, drinking houses,   10
civic affairs, commitments made in unbelief and other things of that kind which are highly regarded by the world and yet are carried on in flat contradiction of God's command . . . Therefore there will unquestionably fall from us the unchristian, devilish weapons of force, such as swords, armour and the like, and all their use, either for one's friends or against enemies – by virtue of the Word of Christ, resist   15
not him that is evil.

(6) We are agreed as follows concerning the sword: the sword is ordained by God outside the perfection of Christ. It punishes and puts to death the wicked and guards and protects the good. In the law the sword was ordained for the punishment of the wicked and for their death, and the same sword is ordained to   20
be used by the worldly magistrates. In the perfection of Christ, however, only the ban is used for a warning and for the excommunication of the one who has sinned, without putting the flesh to death – simply a warning and a command to sin no more. Secondly, it will be asked concerning the sword whether a Christian should pass sentence in worldly disputes and strife such as unbelievers have one with   25
another. This is our united answer: Christ did not wish to pass judgement between brother and brother in the case of inheritance, but refused to do so. Therefore we should do likewise. Thirdly, it will be asked concerning the sword, whether one should be a magistrate if chosen as such. The answer is as follows: they wished to make Christ a king, but he fled and did not see this as the will of his Father. Thus,   30
we shall do as he did and follow him.

(7) We are agreed as follows concerning the oath. The oath is a confirmation among those who are quarrelling and making promises. In the law it is commanded to be performed in God's name, but only in truth, not falsely. Christ, who teaches the perfection of the law, prohibits to his followers all swearing,   35

whether true or false – neither by heaven, nor by the earth, nor by Jerusalem, nor by our own head – and for the reason which he gives shortly thereafter, that you are not able to make one hair black or white. So you see, it is for this reason that all swearing is forbidden: we cannot fulfil that which we promise when we swear, for we cannot change even the very least thing in us.   40

John C. Wenger, 'The Schleitheim Confession of Faith', *Mennonite Quarterly Review*, 19 (1945), pp. 247–51

Questions

1   Why did churchmen and secular authorities regard the Anabaptists as such a threat to Christian order?
2   Were the Anabaptists' beliefs more dangerous in the social and political sphere than in the religious?
3   What were the implications of their views on magistrates and oaths?
4   Was it fair to associate them with Thomas Müntzer's brand of radical religion?
5   How was their radicalism different from his?

6.8   Chiliastic rebellion in Erfurt, 1527

The apocalyptic mood of the year 1527 was marked by the first incident of violent Anabaptist rebellion. At the end of 1527, the town council of Erfurt learned that an armed uprising was planned to take place there on New Year's Day 1528. At first they seemed to have discovered laymen, mainly petty artisans such as shoemakers or furriers, preaching and baptising in the surrounding villages, but as they enquired further they uncovered not only the planned rebellion, fomented and led by Hans Römer, a furrier from Eisenach and disciple of Thomas Müntzer, but a secret network of Anabaptists whose contacts extended throughout most of central Germany. The discovery of the rebellion threw the authorities into panic and sparked off an intensive campaign by the princes of Saxony and the Thuringian nobility to root out the Anabaptist threat, with a level of activity only matched by the campaigns of 1525 against the peasant rebels. The fomenter of the revolt was not apprehended until 1534. The Erfurt chiliastic rebellion was a forerunner of the apocalyptic kingdom of Münster of 1534.

6.8(a)   *Report of the Governor of Langensalza to Duke George of Saxony, 18 December 1527*

On the Saturday before last [7 December], an Erfurt citizen came to the district of Salza and reported that two of the aforesaid fanatics had come to the house of one of his neighbours in Erfurt, and so instructed him in the following articles that he wanted to join their following and go with them.

Infant baptism was false, for Christ said in the Gospel, whoever believes and is   5
baptised, will be saved . . . The old prophetic books should also be translated into German and proclaimed to the common man; these are now being translated by Oecolampadius and Zwingli; and from these one can discover how to deal with secular authority. Christ also said, one should leave house and home, wife and children and follow his Word [cf. Matthew 19]. Whoever will not let himself be   10
baptised again will be consumed by locusts.

Müntzer and Pfeiffer were true teachers and were unjustly slain. And all those who had received the sign of baptism again should wait in the hills, for it would rain locusts, and then the world would not last longer than eleven months.

6.8(b)   *Confession of Hans Römer, Göttingen, 23 September 1534*

Confesses . . . first, that he wanted to have ten bills posted publicly in different places within the city of Erfurt announcing that he intended to preach on Our Lady's Mount [i.e. at the cathedral], so that a crowd would gather in wonderment that a furrier wished to preach, whereupon he would have got up to preach for a week after the bills had been posted. Then, after he had preached, four of his   5
companions, namely Volkmar, Christoph the furrier, Nickel the tailor and the pastor from Alperstedt were to have laid fire in four priests' houses on the Petersberg, and two were to run to the Brühl gate and one to St John's gate, to command in the name of the town council that the gates should not be closed but kept open. Then, when he preached, and as the fire broke out during his   10
preaching, he was to have told the people that the parsons had laid the fire with the intention of preventing the Word of God appearing in the town, and in that way he planned to create a disturbance. When he and his followers could get hold of money, they intended to buy swords and start a peasants' war.

6.8(c)   *Confession of Georg Fuchs, Erfurt, 9 February 1528*

. . . says that it was their intention, when the disturbance broke out in Erfurt, to strike dead whoever was not [re]baptised or would not accept the sign of baptism. Whoever had more than another should share it with him; whoever refused to do so, should also be struck dead (but they expected that the Lutherans would all join them).   5

Confessed that Andres Schneider had said that when the disturbance arose in Erfurt they should go to the Krämpfer gate, which would be opened by Nickel the tailor, and they should all assemble on the Fishmarket and rally to the town hall

and strike dead all the town councillors and other citizens who were not
[re]baptised or would not accept baptism, and seize the city.   10
Scott and Scribner, pp. 328–9 (no. 161)

Questions

1   Summarise the beliefs of those who planned the rebellion in Erfurt.
    How would you characterise their form of evangelical belief?
2   Why did both Lutheran and Catholic authorities agree in condemning
    them?
3   Why do you think they thought it necessary to advance their cause by
    means of a conspiracy?

6.9   The Anabaptists in Münster

The most lurid event in the history of the Reformation was the Anabaptist
Kingdom of Münster. In 1534 Anabaptists won control of the Westphalian
episcopal city, expelled all 'unbelievers', instituted community of goods and
proclaimed the New Jerusalem, the earthly kingdom marking the Last
Days. The subsequent excesses of the bloodthirsty 'King' John of Leiden,
his polygamy and sumptuous court ensured that the Anabaptist kingdom
became a matter of scandal and horror to all contemporaries. It is therefore
difficult to find accounts not written with the polemical intent of denigrat-
ing all that was done by the Münster Anabaptists. The appeal to their
fellow believers to join them at least captures the sense of eschatological
excitement that gripped many Anabaptists at the time.

Appeal of the Anabaptists to come to Münster, early March 1534
Dear brothers and sisters, peace and joy has been granted to the children of God,
for your salvation is at hand. Dear friends, you should know and recognise as the
Word what God has done for us, and each should prepare himself to march to the
new Jerusalem, the city of the saints, for God wants to punish the world. Each
should beware lest he be judged for his inattention. For John Bockelson [of   5
Leiden], the Prophet of Münster, and all his helpers in Christ, has written to us
that no one can remain free under the dragon of this world [i.e. the Antichrist], but
that he will be destroyed either through a bodily or a spiritual death. Therefore no
one should delay joining the march, so that he will not tempt God, for disturbance
is abroad throughout the entire world, and the prophet Jeremiah says in chapter   10
51, flee Babylon so that each might save his soul and your heart may not despair
because of the cries that are abroad throughout the entire land.
      I will tell you nothing more, but I beg you in the name of the Lord to obey
without delay. Take no heed for anything on earth, be it man, woman or child, so

that you will not be deceived. No one should look to their unbelieving children,   15
who are disobedient and are not under the rod, for they are of no use in the
community of the Lord. There is enough property available for the saints. So take
nothing with you other than money, clothing and food for the journey. Whoever
has a knife or pike or musket is to bring it with him, and who does not have these
should buy them, for the Lord will redeem us through his mighty hand . . . No one   20
should delay in coming. If anyone remains behind, I shall be innocent of his blood.

Emanuel.

R van Dülmen, *Das Täuferreich zu Münster 1534–1535*, Munich, 1974,
pp. 78–9

Questions

1   Why does the writer wish to persuade his friends and followers to come
    and join him at Münster? What does he think is going to happen?
2   Why does he advise bringing weapons, yet also say 'Take no heed for
    anything on earth' [line 14]?
3   What does he mean by his reference to 'the saints' [line 4]?
4   Compare this appeal with that made by the Erfurt rebels in 6.8. Were
    they addressing the same aspirations?

6.10   Melchior Hoffman and pacific millennialism

Melchior Hoffman, perhaps the most influential of the early Anabaptists,
began his career in Livonia wholly under the influence of Luther, but later
developed millennialist ideas of his own. His millennialism was pacific,
waiting patiently for the Second Coming. By the 1530s he had begun to see
himself as a prophet of the Last Days, and Strassburg as the city of God
which would witness this event. Harvest failures and other crises in the
years 1527–34 increased the mood of apocalyptic expectation, especially in
Strassburg, with its large Anabaptist community, possibly as many as 500
and allegedly as many as 2,000 in a total population of 20,000. Hoffman's
willingness to set an exact date for the Last Days attracted many followers,
and in 1533 he came to Strassburg, acting on an old Friesian prophecy that
he would suffer imprisonment for six months, after which his teaching
would be spread throughout the entire world. He was indeed arrested in
June 1533, but later changed the date of the prophecy to 1534, then
successively to 1535, 1537 and 1539. The atmosphere of expectation
almost certainly influenced Strassburg to tighten up its previous policy of
tolerance of non-conforming evangelical thought. He was several times
imprisoned and released, but died in prison in 1543, proclaiming to the
end the necessity of obedience to authority while waiting for the End.

23 November 1534: Melchior Hoffman, on his own request, stated the following
to the commissioners: first, he knew that this was the city which God has chosen
above all the cities of the world as his prize; second, that the rulers of this town
would establish his [God's] complete truth . . . On the first point, he knew that all
the old and new prophecies concerning this city had been revealed to his brethren   5
in the Netherlands, but were concealed from this town. He would gladly reveal
them to the city so that it would share this knowledge. For example, when many of
his followers here were driven away, they knew of this action in advance from the
prophecies, and a hundred of them were to be driven out . . . The office of prophet
was now here at hand, as Leonard Jobst indicated, among others. For this reason   10
they did not want to touch him. As proof he cited the example of Jonah, who was
given the task of proclaiming God's judgement over Nineveh.

Quellen zur Geschichte der Wiedertäufer, vol. 8, p. 393 (no. 617)

**John of Leiden Preaching to Anabaptist Followers, from a Low-German Anabaptist
Manuscript, c. 1600.**
All the main descriptions of John of Leiden originate from his enemies, and there
are no contemporary portraits. This drawing from a Low-German Anabaptist
manuscript at least shows him preaching to a wide and attentive congregation
(including children).

Questions

1   How does Hoffman's belief differ from that of the Anabaptists in **6.8**
    and **6.9**? How is it similar?
2   Why was Hoffman, nonetheless, regarded as dangerous enough to
    suffer imprisonment for his beliefs?

6.11   How to deal with Anabaptists, 1536

Following the events at Münster, secular authorities of all kinds became very nervous about Anabaptist activities. However, evangelical authorities were concerned about accusations that they might be persecuting fellow Christians for their belief. Landgrave Philip of Hesse issued a mandate in 1536 ordering the arrest of all suspected Anabaptists in his lands, but at the same time he sought to canvass evangelical opinion about how to treat them, writing to various authorities such as Duke Ernest of Lüneburg, Luther and the other professors at the University of Wittenberg, the Theology Faculties of the universities of Marburg and Tübingen, and the town councils of Strassburg, Augsburg and Ulm. An extract of the reply from Augsburg is reproduced here, revealing much about the attitudes of major imperial cities.

The advisers of the city of Augsburg to the Landgrave, 4 June 1536
We have imprisoned the unpeaceful stirrers and agitators, interrogated them
sternly and well, some of them for incitement and seditious speech, and other
instigators for the disruption of good order and disobedience against the
authorities. But we have punished no one in life and limb chiefly because of their   5
belief, but each according to his guilt, more with the warmest pity than with
severity, flogged them with whips rather than burned them through the cheeks or
even executed them with the sword. For we have had compassion with poor simple
folk who were misled by the leaders, and we sent them off and had our preachers
hold a Christian discourse with them, whereby many were able to recant, and these   10
still live among us in honourable citizen estate. But those who would not let
themselves be instructed by the propounded grounds of Scripture and who
persisted in their error, we have held in prison for as long as they were unwilling to
refrain from such error. Those who then proved stubborn and obstinate for too
long we have exiled from the city with the announcement that it is not because of   15
their belief that they have been cut off from the common citizenry, but because
of their insolence, disobedience and insubordination, so that they would not
poison others besides themselves . . . If they returned and did not immediately
leave again, we imprisoned them again, and racked them in ways equally evil, until
we were finally rid of them.   20

Urkundliche Quellen zur hessischen Reformationsgeschichte, vol. 4,
Marburg, 1951, pp. 104–5

Questions

1   What scruples did the authorities of the city of Augsburg have about
    punishing Anabaptists?
2   What distinctions do they seek to make in dealing with them? What
    main categories of suspects do they use, and how are these justified?

3   Were the Anabaptists being punished for secular reasons and not for their belief?

6.12   The Hessian Estates debate the punishment for Anabaptism, 1536

The various replies from the authorities consulted by Landgrave Philip were read to a committee of the Estates in Kassel on 7 August 1536 and the opinion of each committee member was asked. The replies reveal much of the differing attitudes taken by those of different social status towards the question.

Georg von Kolmatsch Statthalter of Marburg: He could not improve on the views read out, and it would be good to exile the Anabaptists with their goods, and it would be necessary to do so soon. To keep all of them [in prison] would cost a lot. Those who would allow themselves to be exiled could be shown pity, but one should punish some of the stubborn and impious in order to intimidate the others. 5

Johann Feige, Hessian Chancellor. . . . since they were not obedient to authority and wished to have special authorities, and adhered to erroneous seditious doctrines, and would not help defend the fatherland, he thought that they should be dispatched with the sword or other punishment . . . and a common prison should be made for them, where they would be kept until the Almighty 10
enlightened them. But he did not think that they should all be kept together in one place, but separated one from another . . . and that foreigners should be expelled. But when they returned, if they returned for the third time, they should be corporally punished.

Sigmund von Boineburg, County Steward: It pleases him that they first be 15
instructed with the Word; where that is of no help, he first wants to hear the report of the scholars on how and where they should be punished.

Ott Hundt, knight: Since one finds that it concerns not just Anabaptism but other disturbance as well, it is necessary to investigate it and to report first. Also that prayers be said to the Almighty throughout the land to avert such things. But 20
where that was no help, the leaders should be seized and treated as is just; at the same time one can perhaps show grace therein.

Rudolf Schenk, knight: The Anabaptists are not punished for their belief, but because of disturbance and other evil tricks.

Hartman Schleier, knight: They all agreed that they should be instructed by the 25
preachers . . . but those who were exiled and returned should be punished.

Dr Tilman Schnabel, preacher from Alsfeldt: On their errors, they would accept no instruction; no teaching helps and moreover it is no punishment; since they have not previously been punished, the contempt and disorder has flowed from this. On the punishment: when one takes pity on the godless, one gives cause to 30
persist in their ungodliness. One must punish. Can also show grace in this, but no ordinance or command would be observed. Has seen that in Prussia wicked folk must mine metal their life long. One should do so now.

Justus Winther, preacher: Each authority has to force its subjects to hear the Word of God. And the preachers should first treat with the Anabaptists amicably   35
and cordially, so that they will see that one does not seek their goods or blood. Banishment from the land on occasion, or they should go to the mines or work, as has been done before. What concerns punishment, since God has ordained the emperor, one should observe the imperial mandate here.

Fabritius, preacher of Altendorf: Had the bishop, mayor and town council of   40
Münster punished them, the disorder there would have been prevented. And that one should live better and not so unchristianly and pray to God. And thereafter the Anabaptists should be admonished, and where that did not help, they should be punished; for they intended to drive us out all and to set up a new Turkey. Therefore Anabaptism is not at all to be tolerated. A distinction must be observed   45
in the punishment. Exile pleased him, and whoever returned a third time and is then punished is not punished for his belief, but for his disobedience.

Urkundliche Quellen zur hessischen Reformationsgeschichte, vol. 4, pp. 133–6

Questions

1   What fears are expressed in this document about the Anabaptists? What is meant by a 'new Turkey' [**line 44**]?
2   What reasons are given for punishing the Anabaptists?
3   Why were the Anabaptists thought to be stubborn and disobedient?
4   Using a grid diagram, show how the social status and occupation of the speakers affected their attitude to the Anabaptists. What comment would you make on your findings?
5   What kind of punishments are suggested? Rank them in order of severity.
6   Each member of the class take one character and rewrite his speech in your own words. Read the new versions aloud and follow up with a discussion, if possible using role play to sustain the arguments.

6.13   Menno Simons on his conversion

Despite prohibitions and punishments and the reputation visited on the Anabaptists by the events in Münster, many still turned sincerely to that belief. Menno Simons, founder of one of the largest and most peaceful groups, explains much of the Anabaptist mentality in his own account of his conversion.

Dear reader. I write you the truth in Christ and do not lie. In the year 1524, in my twenty-eighth year I entered priestly service in my father's village, called Pinnigum in Friesland, where there were two other priests of the same age. Both of them had read something of Scripture, but I had never touched it in my whole life, for I feared that if I read it I would be led astray. Behold, I was such a stupid preacher 5 for around two years.

The first year thereafter I often thought as I was celebrating the Mass with bread and wine that these were not the flesh and blood of the Lord. I thought that the devil was deceiving me in order to divert me from my faith. I often confessed it, sighed and pleaded, but could not be freed from this thought . . . Finally, I thought 10 that I would diligently explore the New Testament, and I did not get very far in it before I saw that we had been deceived, and my troubled conscience over the aforesaid bread was soon released from this trouble without any human instruction, although I was helped by Luther in this much, that I knew that human commands could not condemn to eternal death. 15

Afterwards it happened, long before I had ever heard of the brethren, that a godfearing pious man called Sicke Snyder was imprisoned in Leeuwarden because he had renewed his baptism. It rang so wonderfully in my ears that someone spoke of a second baptism. I explored the Scripture with diligence and reflected on it in earnest, but could find no report of infant baptism. Now when I noted this, I had a 20 discussion with my pastor on this subject and brought him so far in as many words that he had to confess that infant baptism had no ground in Scripture. At the same time, I did not trust my own understanding alone, but sought advice in several authors who taught that children had to be cleansed from their original sin. I compared this with Scripture and found that this was contrary to the blood of 25 Christ.

Next the sect at Münster befell us, which deceived many pious hearts. My soul was in great affliction, for I recognised that they were zealous but were deceived in their doctrine. I opposed them in sermons and admonitions as much as I was able with my small talents. I had two discussions with one of their elders, one in secret, 30 the second publicly, but my admonitions had no success . . . The rumour went around, near and far, that I could neatly shut the mouths of these people. They all invoked me, whoever they were, so that I could see with my own eyes how I was a defender and citadel for the impenitent, who all relied on me, which was no small blow to my heart, so that I sighed and prayed, Lord help me so that I will not take 35 the sins of others upon myself . . . With this consideration, my soul so gnawed at me that I could stand it no longer. I thought to myself: what shall I do, poor miserable creature? If I remain with the old church and do not quicken the Word of the Lord with my acquired knowledge; if I do not rebuke with the Word of the Lord the hypocrisy of the learned and the impenitent fleshly life and their 40 perverted baptism, communion and worship according to my small talents . . . ah, then how much blood would be shed.

I began to teach publicly from the pulpit in the name of the Lord the Word of true repentance; to point the people to the narrow path, to rebuke by the strength of the Word all sins and godlessness, as well as all idolatry and false worship; to 45 bear witness publicly to the true divine worship, baptism and communion, according to the sense of the doctrine of Christ, according to the degree of the grace I had at that time received from God.

Hillerbrand, *Reformation in its Own Words*, pp. 266–70

Questions

1 What picture does Menno Simons give of his life as a young Catholic priest?
2 How did he come to change his religious beliefs? What new beliefs did he adopt?
3 How was he influenced by Luther and how far was he thus influenced?
4 What brought about his final breach with the Catholic church?
5 How closely do Simons' beliefs accord with those of the Schleitheim Confession (**6.8**)? In what sense was he an Anabaptist?
6 Why do you think he was so opposed to the Anabaptists of Münster?

6.14   The Hutterites in Moravia

From 1526, Anabaptists, fleeing persecution and putting into practice their belief in separation from the ungodliness of the world, began to migrate to areas where they found more tolerant authorities, most notably in Moravia. Balthasar Hubmeier led the way, in 1526 converting to Anabaptism a local nobleman, Leonhard von Liechtenstein, whose seat at Nikolsburg became a centre of Moravian Anabaptism. In 1527 Hans Hut came to Moravia, and it was his fervent advocacy of the principles of non-resistance that gave the group its distinctive stance. The belief in community of goods of another founder of the colony, Jacob Wiedemann, provided the other distinctive doctrine of the Moravian Anabaptists. The first redistribution of property occurred in 1528, as Leonhard von Liechtenstein took fright at the fear of imperial prosecution and the Anabaptists were forced to leave Nikolsburg and seek refuge on the lands of another nobleman. The Hutterites derived their name, however, from their first leader, the Tyrolean Anabaptist Jacob Hutter, who arrived in Moravia in 1533.

The first community of goods, 1528
Therefore they sought to sell their possessions. Some sold, but others simply abandoned them, and they departed with one another from thence. Whatever remained of theirs the lord of Liechtenstein sent after them. So around two hundred persons, without counting children, from Nikolsburg, Bergen and the vicinity gathered before the town. Some of the citizens went out to them and wept   5
with great compassion for them, but others argued with them. However, they set out for the district between Tannewitz and Muschau, and struck camp in a deserted village, where they remained for a day and a night while they ook counsel in the Lord what to do . . . Someone spread out a coat on the ground and each placed his or her wealth in it, voluntarily and with a willing heart, for the support   10

of the needy, according to the teaching of the prophets and Apostles (Isaiah 23:18, Acts 2, 4 and 5).

Hillerbrand, *Reformation in its Own Words*, pp. 270–1

6.15   Life in a Hutterite community, 1578

The following account, written by a visitor from Württemberg who went to see his relatives in Moravia, gives some impression of life in a Hutterite community, as well as of the Hutterite mentality, which often irritated outsiders, who found it too pious or even arrogant.

On the 22nd . . . as we set out for Stignitz, my sister Margaret and my brother-in-law Michael talked to me of the natural love and inclination with which they had often thought of me, and of how they had often wished me to be present there. And I told them that since the last time they had never been out of my thoughts, and that I had always remembered them to God in my prayers. Then   5
Christman, the husband of my sister Margaret, spoke up and said that I should not pray for him, for God did not hear the prayers of the godless but regarded them as a sin. I could neither wish nor gain him anything good.

I found at Stignitz my other sister, who was married to a vintner, and who keeps the children tidy in their Anabaptist school. For each Anabaptist dwelling has a   10
school in which the children are placed from the age of two years (until which they remain with their mothers), so that they might learn to pray and to read, although they study no further. The girls usually learn only to pray and to write a little, but the boys learn to write and to read, until they are older, when they are set to learn a trade or to do some other work. The children each day go often into the fields or   15
into the nearby woods, so that they are not continually crowded together, but may get some fresh air.

The children are assigned specific women who do nothing other than to take care of them, wash them, look after them, and keep their bedding and clothes clean and fresh. The children sleep two to a bed. Each morning and evening they   20
hold prayers that God will let them be brought up to fear him and grant them good folk who will educate them in knowledge of him, and that their brothers and sisters in the fields will be protected from all accidents. After this prayer, which they say on their knees, they recite the Lord's Prayer.

My sister Sara did not take her husband gladly, but she could say nothing   25
against this, for they arrange their marriages as follows: the elders on a certain Sunday summon all the youths and maidens of marriageable age to them in a particular dwelling, introduce them one to another, and present two or three youths to each maiden from whom she has to choose. She has to take one of them, and although she is not forced to do so, she may not act contrary to the elders.   30

I met my half-brother Sebastian at the brewery, but he did not want to shake hands with me at first, just as Christman had previously done. His first words were that I was a false prophet, so that he could not shake my hand . . . On the 23rd an elder came to me and . . . began to speak to me of the Christian church, saying that many boast of being Christians who are not at all so, because they perform no good 35 works: one would know the tree by its fruit. He said that there were downright godless folk in the world, and much dissension and many sects among us, but that they had left all that behind and had followed Christ. Finally he began to speak of community of property and wanted to prove this from 1 Cor. 10:24.

Hillerbrand, *Reformation in its Own Words*, pp. 271–3

Questions

1   What were the characteristics of Hutterite belief as set out in **6.14** and **6.15**?
2   Why were the Hutterites allowed to set up new communities in Moravia? Why did they prove to be more lasting than those in Germany or Switzerland?
3   Look at **6.15** and make a list of the author's relatives and their differing attitudes towards him. How had Anabaptist belief changed family relationships?
4   What evidence does **6.15** provide about
    (a) communal living
    (b) education
    (c) authority within the community
    (d) treatment of females?
5   How does this Anabaptist group compare to others in this chapter?

7 The consolidation of reform

The Reformation is often described merely as the preaching of new religious ideas and the abolition of the Catholic church. However, it was a major part of reform to construct new institutions and develop new forms of church life. This was not seen as a problem at first. Luther and many who thought like him did not accept that there was a schism in the church, and gave little thought to the question of reorganisation. Indeed, Luther believed this to be an idle question, since he expected the Last Days and the end of the world within his lifetime. Thus, in Lutheran areas, reform was institutionalised in piecemeal and makeshift fashion. For want of anyone else to carry it out, this fell into the willing hands of secular rulers. What began in electoral Saxony as an emergency measure became a basis for permanent institutions, and because it was not at first well thought out, it was slow and lacked success. The attempt to spread reform to all levels of society also encountered resistance from a predominantly rural population still attached to its traditional forms of thought and behaviour. Moreover, the initial idealistic belief of the reformers that their reformation would lead to the creation of a pious Christian people was quickly shattered by the reality of human nature. It was not long before old conflicts resurfaced in new guise, while new ones were added.

7.1 Instruction for the visitors in electoral Saxony

The rapid pace of religious reform, often undertaken on local initiative, threatened to plunge the church into chaos. The idea that the secular ruler should take charge of religious reform of the church in order to prevent disintegration was first suggested in May 1525, in the wake of the peasant rebellion. Luther later added his support for this idea, thinking at first only of the removal of unsuitable clergy and a reshaping of financial provision in the parishes. In June 1527 Elector John the Constant ordered such a visitation, although no doctrinal questions were mentioned. The addition of a thorough review of doctrine and religious practice was worked out in discussions among theologians in Wittenberg (Luther, Melanchthon, Bugenhagen, Spalatin), who produced a thick book of instructions informing the visitors on the points they were to investigate. The following extracts from the preface seek to provide a justification for this undoubtedly secular intervention in the affairs of the church, especially by depicting the degeneration of church government under papal rule into money-grubbing and tyranny.

That it is a godly and holy work for suitably instructed persons to visit the pastors and Christian communities is shown in both the New and Old Testaments, for we see that St Paul travelled around in the Jewish lands, Acts 9:32, 38f . . . as did Elijah and Eliseus, as we can read in the Book of Kings [2 Kings 2: 1–6] . . . This example was also followed by the ancient fathers of the church, the holy bishops of 5 early times, about which much can be found in papist laws. The bishops and archbishops originally developed from this activity, in which each was ordered to visit and inspect each pastor and his flock and to supervise their life and doctrine, for 'bishop' actually means 'supervisor' or 'visitor', and an archbishop is the supervisor of such visitors . . . In the course of time the office of bishop became a 10 haughty secular lordship, while the bishops made themselves into lords and rulers and thought it beneath them to do such things and entrusted it to provosts, deans and cathedral canons. Afterwards, the provosts, deans and canons turned into lazy gentry, and entrusted the task to officials, who plagued the land with citations before the church courts for the sake of money and visited no one. Finally, things 15 went even further downhill and got even worse, for the officials remained at home in their warm parlours and sent some rogue or knave out into the countryside and the towns, who ran around listening to the bad-mouthed gossip in the inns about individual men or women, which he then reported to the official, who then attacked them through his butcher's office and flayed them of their money, even 20 the innocent, and deprived them of reputation and honour . . . In sum, such holy work has collapsed and nothing has remained of it.

Now that the Gospel has been mercifully restored to us by the ineffable grace of God . . . from which we have seen how miserably Christendom has been scattered, tattered and torn, we would willingly have seen the proper office of bishop and 25 visitor re-established as something highly necessary. But none of us is called to do so or has any explicit command, and St Peter would allow nothing to be done in Christendom unless it is certain that it is the work of God, so none of us dared to set himself up above another. Thus we wanted to be sure in conscience and to turn to that office of love which is commanded to all Christian communities [i.e. to the 30 Christian authority]. So we have humbly petitioned his excellency, the most highborn prince and lord John, duke of Saxony, High Marshall and Elector of the Holy Roman Empire . . . as our territorial prince and our secular authority ordained by God, that his princely grace would appoint some skilled persons to this office out of Christian love (for he is not obliged to do so from his secular 35 authority), for the sake of God, the good of the Gospel and of suffering Christians, which his princely grace has done, with God's approval, and appointed four persons [Hans von der Planitz, knight, Hieronymus Schurff, doctor of canon and civil law, Master Philip Melanchthon and the official Asmus von Haubitz] . . . God grant that it will give a blessed example and that all other German princes may fruitfully imitate it.   40

Sehling, *Die evangelischen Kirchenordnungen des xvi. Jhts*, vol. 1/i, pp. 149–51

Questions

1   How in 7.1 was the intervention of a secular ruler in the affairs of the church justified?
2   What account does the document give of the origins of bishops and of the decline of the office?
3   How, according to this account, is this process related to the origins of the Reformation?
4   Consider the kinds of person appointed to conduct the visitation. What does this tell us about the nature of the exercise?

7.2   The problem of an adequate clergy: the Reformation in Ulm, 1531

When the town council of Ulm decided formally to introduce religious reform in 1531, it summoned all the clergy in the town and the Ulm territories to a hearing at the town hall. They were presented with eighteen articles embodying the Ulm Reformation and asked whether they agreed with them or preferred to uphold the 1530 imperial recess of Augsburg condemning heresy. The replies of the one hundred persons questioned (35 in the town, 65 in the countryside) are the most detailed source we have for the views of the clergy in a major imperial city and its territory. It is surprising how few of them, especially the rural clergy, had any real understanding of the issues, despite evangelical ideas having been preached in and around Ulm for almost a decade. However, for want of anyone suitable to replace them, all but those most recalcitrant and unwilling to change were retained in office. Because the full list is too long to reproduce in its entirety, representative replies from a fifth of the total questioned are given here. The document reveals vividly the difficulty of introducing reform without an adequate clergy.

Examination of the clergy within the city, Monday 5 June 1531
    [5] *Gori Greckh*: he has no skill in the matter; will remain in his calling until all believers recognise what should be believed. That's what he would do. He is too unimportant to dispute about these matters without an assembly [i.e. a General Council] of the church.

[8] *Cristan Hezeler*: will stand by that which has been handed down to him for   5
eleven or twelve hundred years; he is too unimportant either to object to or to
confirm the Articles.

[15] *Bernhart Neithart*: will hold whatever pleases the worthy town council. He
can say nothing of the Articles, because he does not understand the matter.

[17] *Dr Wilhelm Rot*: will behave towards the worthy town council as is required,   10
just the same as any other secular citizen, and will uphold the Articles. Does not
know how to improve on the worthy town council's views. He became a priest from
poverty; wished that it had never happened. Asked to be given the protection of the
worthy town council.

[18] *Martin Idelhauser*: has long since taught what the Articles say and had   15
expounded them to [Martin] Bucer; he had only disagreed with the others on the
Mass, but is now content.

[21] *Conrad Kollin*: he too is worthless. He commends the matter to God and the
assembled authorities. (He also said to the city constable, Hans Stork, that he
should pray to God for him that they would not cut off his balls.)   20

[34] *Hans Villicus*: will remain by the old usage, as [do] those from
Westerstetten; his father taught him so and asked him to become a priest; he will
remain by it, whether he go to the devil or not.

Many were afterwards sent for again.

Examination of all priests in the territory, Wednesday, 7 June 1531

[38] *Johannes Mann*, chaplain at Reutti: formerly had a wife and has been a   25
priest for twelve years; previously he learned much at the schools [and] at the papal
and episcopal courts during the time when he was a priest and followed the
[papist] beliefs, but has been partly enlightened for about two years and has partly
given them up. He is pleased with the Articles.

[39] *Hans Zimmermann*, chaplain at Geislingen (endowed by the court at   30
Geislingen): he has not understood the Articles; what the worthy town council
thought good pleased him too. He believed what the Christian church, that is the
approved [General] Councils, believed. He also held that the Mass was right.

[41] *Martin Salzlin*, parson at Byningen (endowed by the Carthusians of
Buchsheim): Paul says at the end of the [Epistle to the] Hebrews, let yourself not   35
be deceived by false teaching; therefore he must understand whether the Articles
are false teaching and for this he needs time. Further, Paul says in Romans 13 one
must be obedient to the authorities; he must, therefore, in fairness be obedient to
his bishop, to whom he has sworn obedience, and so must look to him for his
understanding.   40

[44] *Hans Widemann*, parson at Sontbergen (endowed by the town council):
considers the Articles to be Christian, though has not the skill to defend them;
previously held the Mass to be good, but is willing to be told better.

[49] *Jeorius Bretzel*, parson at Radelstetten: it is too difficult for him to judge the
Articles when the scholars themselves cannot agree. Begs that he be allowed to   45
remain by that which he has formerly taught and by the Roman church, until a
[General] Council. Is greatly confused on the Mass and the Sacrament.

[55] *Weiler of Helfenstein* (endowed by the provost of Herwartingen): will remain by what he has previously taught; will leave it to the scholars, knows nothing of it.

[64] *Parson of Lonsee* (endowed by the abbot of Blaubeuren): he is a simple man   50 and can say nothing about the matter, since the doctors themselves quarrel over it. His abbot has commanded him to teach the old faith; the majority of the Articles please him; he is troubled only about the Sacrament.

[75] *Parson at Naw*: holds the majority of Articles for Christian, and has also taught them; will consider the others.   55

[81] *Jakob (Jorg) Stehlen*, chaplain at Leipheim: holds them to be neither Christian nor unchristian.

[84] *Hans Siler*, chaplain to Aufhausen: will pass the Articles to my lords [of the town council] to judge, and will do what the worthy town council asks.

[85] *Michael Graeb*, parson at Holzschwang: will neither criticise nor praise the   60 Articles and will remain a priest. He would not hide the fact that he once said that it was a rag-tag belief, but he did not believe in the present [old] belief. He was ordered to read only the text of the Epistle and Gospel from the book without any exposition.

[91] *Johannes Kalhart*, parson of Amstetten: the Articles are against his belief; he   65 remains by the town council.

[99] *Jorg Geyss*, administrator of the parish of Siessen (presented by the abbot of Adelsberg): the Articles please him indeed, for he has preached the majority of them.

G. Keidel, 'Ulmische Reformationsakten von 1531 und 1532', *Württembergische Vierteljahrshcft für Landesgeschichte*, NF4 (1895) pp. 260–3, 265–9

Questions

1   Treating 7.2 as if it were an opinion poll, work out the percentage replies for the following questions (there are twenty replies listed):
    (a) How many understood the issues of the Reformation?
    (b) How many supported it unconditionally?
    (c) How many opposed it on firm religious or doctrinal grounds?
    (d) How many supported it because the secular authority did so?
    (e) How many gave conditional approval?
    (f) List the different kinds of condition.
2   Why did so many of the clergy refer to a General Council of the church as the means of settling the doctrinal dispute?
3   What does this document tell you about the reception of Reformation ideas among the clergy?
4   What can you deduce from the document about the reception of these ideas among laypeople?

7.3 Visitations as a means of reform

The difficulties of implementing religious reform with an inadequate clergy and a recalcitrant peasantry can be seen in the following extracts from the 1529 Saxon visitation in the district of Schweinitz.

Plossick (20 leaseholders, 15 cottagers). It is rumoured that the pastor is suspect of papist usages and doctrines, but almost a year ago he went over to the Gospel. Has few books, promises improvement and is placed under the supervision of the pastor of Prettin, who shall keep an eye on his diligence and doctrines, and if he is found to be lazy or inconstant it should be reported to the Visitors or the district   5
official, so that the people can be provided with another pastor.

Aryn (18 householders). The pastor, Rev. Martinus Mauck. [On the question as to whether he was evangelical and administered Communion under both kinds:] we have reports to the contrary, that he teaches untruths, and that he still secretly uses blessed water. In sum, through rumour and reports from the people, he has   10
been found to be still quite a papist; therefore, we have dismissed him.

Lebbyn (16 leaseholders, 2 cottagers). The pastor is quite unskilled, and does not know himself what to do, follows both the old and the new way, and has therefore been dismissed.

Stolzenhayn (16 leaseholders, 6 cottagers). The pastor submitted a letter   15
concerning several abominable crimes and blasphemies which the folk in Stolzenhayn demonstrated against the Word of God and divine worship . . . The folk have been earnestly admonished to repentance . . . The people in Stolzenhayn have also withheld their tithe from the pastor, of which he receives one-third, while two-thirds go to our gracious lord [the Elector].   20

Loben (16 householders, 12 farmers). The pastor is poorly educated and is unsuitable to serve the folk. Therefore another has been deputed to reside in his house for four weeks, with bed and board, and to instruct him and the people. At the end of these four weeks, if the parson is somewhat instructed and he undertakes to be more diligent and careful, he is to preach the Gospel on Sundays   25
and [teach] the Catechism during the week as long as he lives or remains there.

Holzdorf. The pastor complains that the effort he makes in preaching is despised by the people. He had undertaken to preach twice during the week but had to give up because of their indifference. There was more than enough sorcery, adultery and other vices, but the peasants wanted to go unpunished. There was in   30
particular a sorceress called Hermanin, who told the folk where they could find anything they had lost. His churchwarden's wife was a public adulteress, and to spite him the peasants took her part. Nonetheless, we have dismissed the pastor, who is to depart by Easter.

Dubro. The people in the two parishes Holzendorf and Dubro are quite wicked   35
and wanton. They heed no advice, unless it comes from the hangman or the gaoler and unless they were [threatened with being] driven away and other pious folk settled there. However, they have been given a pastor to care for their souls.

Wertho (14 leaseholders, 1 cottager). The peasants here neither pray, nor believe nor know the Ten Commandments properly, nor have they previously taken the   40

blessed Sacrament. So the pastor is to allow no one to take Communion unless he
or she has first been confronted with his or her sins and confesses them and can
answer the five questions [on the faith].

Wildenau (23 householders, including 17 leaseholders). The peasants can pray
quite well and they praise their pastor as someone who is quite learned. The local   45
noblewoman would like to have a different pastor, and has heard an accusation
from someone from Tenstedt that he refused to administer the Sacrament under
both kinds. But the peasants reported on him rather differently, in the presence of
the noblewoman's servants.

Treben. Things are done here with much contempt and wickedness. In five years   50
very few have taken Communion. The solemn feast of the Ascension is not
celebrated at all. Yet the pastor rejoices in, and loves, the pure doctrine of the holy
Gospel, and the nobility speak well of him in all things concerning the Gospel.
The nobility and the peasants were spoken to earnestly and admonished to
improvement. The pastor has preached only on Sundays and has not celebrated   55
Mass because of lack of communicants, so that he was ordered to hold divine
worship.

**Staatsarchiv Dresden, loc. 10598, 'Registration der Visitation etlicher
Sächsischen, Meissnischen Kreise, Ämter, 1529'**

Questions

1   List the main difficulties hindering the progress of reform in the
    district of Schweinitz.
2   Which do you think were the most serious hindrances?
3   How far did social position influence willingness to accept reform?
4   Assess the degree of success of reform in the district.
5   How was this to be remedied?

7.4   Dissolution of the monasteries

The main problem in setting up a new church organisation was to provide
adequate financial support. Many of the old clergy had drawn their
incomes from pious foundations based on belief in salvation through good
works. The new churches could not rely on such sources of income, while
the old church endowments had suffered erosion in the course of time by
inflation or dissipation. One possibility was to dissolve monastic institutions
and devote their incomes to the upkeep of the new church, paying the
clergy's salaries from them and devoting the remainder to the support of
the poor. However, monasteries had in the past fulfilled a valuable role as
welfare institutions for the unmarried children of the nobility, and many
nobles were unwilling to give this up. An interesting solution was found in
Hesse. Although the nobility was suspicious of the landgrave – fearing he

sought to gain control of the resulting incomes – attempts to check this proved inadequate, for the supervisory committee never met.

Dissolution of the monasteries by the Hessian Territorial Diet, 1527
[After the imperial Diet of Speyer of 1526 declared] that each ruler may in his lands and territories so act and determine as he considers he can answer before God and his imperial majesty, we [Landgrave Philip of Hesse] summoned [representatives] from our towns and nobility and agreed to deal with the monasteries and religious orders as follows: 5

   1 . . . whoever wishes to leave [the cloister] shall be given a fair payment on discharge, [the nobles receiving either the full wealth they brought in with them or a minimum of 100 florins, others according to their circumstances]. Whoever wishes to remain will receive the necessary support, the women will be sent to a suitable place and the men to the Kugelhaus in Marburg, so that they may study in   10
a college.
   2 [The landgrave] intends that two monasteries should be established in the upper and lower parts of the principality, in which the nobility should maintain their children, [fifty in each place. If the nobility think it preferable to place the incomes in a common chest from which eight nobles might be paid 200–300   15
florins a year each, he would also permit that.].
   [He also desires that thirty nobles, fifteen each in both parts of the principality] should be provided in their dwellings with some incomes in corn, wheat and oats, so that they might remain under arms.
   3 We wish to support the University of Marburg from the monastic incomes.   20
   4 [All other remaining monastic incomes] shall fall to a common chest, supervised by two of our councillors, two appointees from the nobility and two from the towns. [The officers appointed to run the chest shall provide them with an annual accounting, so that when there is need in the land] the money shall be used to support the poor and the land not so exhausted with taxation.   25

Urkundliche Quellen zur hessischen Reformationsgeschichte, vol. 2, p. 45

7.5   The re-establishment of church discipline

The rulers of the newly established territorial church were determined not to allow the social and religious indiscipline of the early reform movements to continue within the new church polity. This was to be achieved by enforcing strict rules of behaviour towards the new clergy and doctrines, as revealed in the 1533 ecclesiastical statutes for electoral Saxony. The desire for discipline even led to the reintroduction of practices whose removal had constituted the touchstone of the 'Christian freedom' of the early Reformation, as occurred in Brandenburg, where fast and abstinence from meat was retained for disciplinary reasons.

7.5(a)   *The Saxon Church Statutes of 1533*

The authorities, officials, castellans, knights and nobility, as well as the councillors in the towns are diligently to admonish their subjects, and exhort them to attend sermons and other divine services, to pray to God for his grace, to hear his holy Word diligently and to keep it.

No one is to speak to the parson or preacher while he is in the pulpit; but if   5
anyone does not understand the preacher, he should go alone to the parson or preacher, and converse with him amicably and pleasantly. The parson or preacher should instruct such a person amicably, and where they cannot settle the matter, they should go to the superintendent and let themselves be instructed.

Sehling, *Die evangelischen Kirchenordnungen des xvi. Jhts*, vol. 1/i, p. 187

7.5(b)   *The Brandenburg Church Statutes of 1540*

On fasting

As a territorial prince and father of the fatherland, we have the power, after taking good advice, to issue political statutes that serve the common good, provided that the conscience is not bound before God; also so that the young and ignorant folk become accustomed to moderation. Now since Christ ordained no specific times [for fasting] nor made no distinction in food, it is therefore unjust to make specific   5
laws which bind the conscience . . . contrary to God's Word and Christian freedom. However, the Lord himself taught us that we should live soberly and moderately, and control the body so that it will be made obedient to the spirit, just as the Apostles did, what is called 'fasting' in Scripture. Now since the young and the common folk are too ignorant and inclined to excess, if one did not compel   10
them to do so, they would not learn moderation and would fall into excessive gorging and guzzling; so it is fitting that the secular authority consider passing statutes which each father of a household should make his servants observe.

Now since it is not suitable to enact new special times [for fasting], it is more convenient to retain those which have been customary, namely Friday and   15
Saturday each week and the forty days of Lent. And since meat is out of season during Lent and our principality of Brandenburg is well supplied with fish, it is not unreasonable to ordain that throughout this period the communities should abstain from meat. Further, the wicked miscreants, of whom there are many in every place, who want to attack the Gospel in any way by gorging and guzzling,   20
purely to spite the authorities, to disconcert good police and as a scandal to the weak, should be punished in order not thoughtlessly and needlessly to hinder the Gospel in other places.

But it is proper to instruct the people diligently that the conscience is in no way to be bound by such times [of fasting] or distinction of food, nor made sinful   25
before God, except for mischievous wickedness and scandal, for to prohibit foods is, as Paul says to Timothy [1 Tim. 4:3], diabolical and leads astray. But pregnant women, the sick or the sickly shall use their Christian freedom unhindered.

Sehling, *Die evangelischen Kirchenordnungen des xvi. Jhts*, vol. 3, p. 87

7.6   Working of the new church

The difficulties of training suitable pastors, of relations between clergy and parishioners, and of maintaining the boundaries between the two realms of the spiritual and secular within a state church, meant that the new Lutheran churches did not experience smooth and untroubled progress, as shown by the following documents. **7.6** also shows the importance of a ceremony of ordination in the new Lutheran church, despite the theoretical abolition of distinctions between clergy and laity.

Report of the examiners appointed in Weimar to ordain pastors, 1551
[They are aggrieved that very young men are sent to them for examination and ordination] for the peasants and others abuse their youth and despise their teaching and sermons of reproof because of their youth. The young folk also [recognise this] and nothing can be done with them; they begin to gamble, to carouse, to dance and to carry on with other disorder. Thus, for reasons of the   5
status of the pastors in this high office, it is fitting that they should be left to study longer and to lay down a better basis for the office of preacher; or the opportunity taken for them to be deacons alongside an experienced pastor.

Furthermore, none should be sent here by their superintendent unless they first

Luther and the Elector John Frederick of Saxony before a Crucifix.
The depiction commemorates Luther as the originator of reform, emphasising
both the central Lutheran doctrine of reliance on Christ alone and Lutheranism's
dependence on princely protection. Such illustrations resembled traditional
altarpieces or devotional images and served to strengthen solidarity among
evangelical believers.

possess at least a German Bible and the Postils of Dr Martin Luther of holy   10
memory, for they seldom acquire them afterwards. After all, a soldier must have
his weapons and armour before he signs up. Then there is their dress, which is
poorly worn in the ministry: they should have a respectable coat and not one
fashionably cut, for many of them arrive looking like rogues, and we have had to
lend them clothes out of shame, for whoever turns to the ministry should have   15
reasonable, worthy and untattered clothing.

Many are ordained as deacons and as simple village parsons (as the saying goes,
no doctor would let himself be sent to such a position), but once they are ordained
they immediately begin to think of higher things, which seems unsuitable to us and
for which we can give no testimonial. In case they do not devote enough diligence   20
to their books, as is customary, [and want to seek a new position] they should come
to be examined again and show cause for such a change, and show that they have
improved themselves and are adequate for the church to which they are to be
called.

Staatsarchiv Weimar Reg. Ii 2261

Questions

1   How did the Reformation change the relationship between clergy and
    laypeople? (Refer to 7.5 and 7.6.)
2   How did the new clergy differ from the old? (See 7.6.)
3   What greater control did the secular ruler have over the new clergy?
    (See 7.4 and 7.5.)
4   How did this benefit lay Christians?
5   What benefits did the secular ruler derive from the new arrangements?
6   What did 'Christian freedom' mean in the new churches? (See 7.5(b).)

7.7   Disputes over the right of communities to elect their pastors

One of the fundamental tenets of early evangelical belief was the right of
communities to elect their own pastors. This right was often lost as the
territorial prince took charge of church life. Pastors were appointed by the
prince or his officials, and communities given only the passive right to
consent to or refuse the appointment. The real test of this principle came
when communities wished to dismiss an unsuitable pastor. This occurred
in exemplary fashion in the Saxon village of Rinkleben in 1564, where the
villagers laid complaints against their irascible pastor Phillip Schmidt,
finally securing his dismissal. They then attempted to choose their own
pastor in accordance with evangelical doctrine. The exchange of views on
this occasion sets out the different positions in such disputes, and reveals
that it was not always concern for the Word of God that played the leading
role.

7.7(a)   The community of Rinkleben to the duke of Saxony, 20 April 1564

Eight years ago our present pastor was appointed to the cure of souls here in Rinkleben, albeit without our call or consent. Now, he has behaved so strangely, irascibly and troublesomely and dealt with us in such fashion that he has neglected his office . . . so that we have been little edified by his teaching or conduct. We can no longer be patient or stand silent as we have hitherto done . . . [a list of seventeen 5 complaints follows] . . . so we humbly beseech your grace to provide us with another pious, learned, loyal and diligent pastor.

7.7(b)   Reply of Phillip Schmidt, pastor of Rinkleben, to the duke of Saxony

It is true that I was appointed [and not called by them, but] this appointment was made by your grace and your appointed Visitors . . . Now they want to make this an irregular appointment . . . because they were not consulted and had no part in it. Is this not a devilish calumny, to impugn a pastor appointed, confirmed and tested in office for almost nine years by God and high authority? Is that not wickedly and 5 knowingly to set themselves up against your grace's ordinances and confirmation? . . . Your grace can deduce from this not only what my parishioners but also all peasants in this principality and in others really want. They want to have the right of electing, calling, confirming and deposing their spiritual shepherd just as they do with their cowherd and shepherd . . . And if the call was conducted 10 according to the will of those of Rinkleben, they would have shamelessly chosen a good eating and drinking chum . . . or a pious antinomian honey-preacher.

7.7(c)   The community of Rinkleben to the superintendent of Weimar, 8 June 1568

[You will recall the problems we had with our previous pastor who was forced upon us against our will.] Now we are informed that our gracious prince, the duke of Saxony, has allowed every community the right to call its own pastors, and we want to remind your grace of this fact . . . We are writing to announce that we therefore wish to choose our schoolmaster as our new pastor.   5

7.7(d)   Reports of the official of Rinkleben, Georg Wolrab

To Bartholomeus Rosinus, superintendent of Weimar, 16 June 1568: [He corrects the notion that he approves of the election.] For certain members of the community have undertaken to retain [control of] the parish, and intrigue and keep the matter so secret that one of the headmen and a third of the community, as well as myself . . . have not hitherto been aware of it . . . They want to have the 5 schoolmaster so that they will not have to pay him school fees. All this has been set afoot by the most prominent peasants, the village officials and the large farmers, who are also pushing it so strongly; . . . they want to be as wilful as the free Swiss.

To his brother-in-law, ducal secretary in Weimar, 18 June 1568: [Asks him to
intervene so that the schoolmaster will not be appointed] so that the peasants will   10
not get their own way . . . I would suggest the chaplain of Buttelstedt, Martin
Christian . . . but if the peasants know that I want him, then they will not accept
him.

Undated report from Wolrab: The ducal councillors have sent the new pastor of
Rinkleben to hold a trial sermon here, but the peasants do not want to have him.   15
They can give no reason for this except that he would have made less fuss about
loose living for the bigwigs than for the peasants and would not doff his cap to
these rude fellows. But when I wanted to report this to my gracious lord [the
duke], they called him to the post. You can imagine what kind of wicked folk
they are!   20

Staatsarchiv Weimar, Reg. Ll 670, 671

Questions

1   Summarise the different views about appointing a pastor revealed in
     7.7.
2   What issues played a part in the appointment?
3   Comment on Schmidt's claim about what the peasants 'really' wanted?
4   Discuss in class how you would have resolved the problem at a meeting
     of princely councillors.

7.8   Philip Melanchthon on the different reasons for supporting the Gospel

As the first generation of reform neared its end, it had become clear that
support for the Gospel was very mixed, and arose from very mixed motives,
including self-interest and the desire to gain political advantage. Philip
Melanchthon showed his awareness of this in a private letter to Chilian
Goldstein of 2 April 1545.

'Many are called but few are chosen.' The theologians dispute over many and
various interpretations of this saying but I think a simple explanation can be given
according to the four categories enumerated by Aristotle.

1 Some love the Gospel naturally, that is they hate the chains of laws and
ceremonies, and on the other hand love the relaxation of discipline; for which   5
reason they believe the Gospel to be a short and direct way of gaining the freedom
to throw off all burdens, by which blind desire they are brought to love of the
Gospel. In this first category can be included the greater part of the common folk
who are ignorant of the basis of doctrine and the origins of controversies, and they
regard the way of the Gospel as cattle regard a new gateway [i.e. something to shy   10
away from].

2 However there are others, among them many great and noble persons, who form their views of religion in the manner of Jezabel, according to the moods of present-day rulers. There are many such persons at princely courts just now who approve this or that religion not because they really think that way, but because   15
they are unwilling to offend the views of princes.

3 There are others who display great diligence in piety and singular zeal, but they attempt under this pretext to satisfy their own passions. Many soft-living persons belong in this category.

4 The last category contains the true elect, that is those who judge the main   20
controversies with a right mind and are aware of their basis, and whose will is so confirmed by the Holy Spirit that they do not doubt that all human affairs could be lost for confessing divinely taught doctrine. Christ was undoubtedly speaking of their perseverance, which falls only to a few. For he did not wish to make any particular election, but to distinguish degrees of hearing the Gospel and to assess   25
them not from outward appearance, of which nothing is more uncertain or deceptive, but on inner grounds, that is in mind and will.

Corpus Reformatorum, vol. 5, pp. 725–6.

Questions

1 Summarise in your own words the four categories identified by Melanchthon.

2 How did the different reasons for supporting the Gospel influence the progress of reform?

Ein Chriſtlich Teſtament vnnd Seliges Abſterben des Heiligen Confeſſoris oder Bekenners
Chriſti vnnd ſeines Euangelij / Johann Friedrichs Hertzog zu Sachſſen.

Memorial Sheet for Duke John Frederick of Saxony, by Pangratz Kempf, 1554. This sheet depicts the near hagiographic reverence attached after his death to the Elector John Frederick, who was hailed as a Lutheran saint and martyr because of his imprisonment after defeat in the first Schmalkaldic War. He is shown here receiving a vision of the crucified Christ as Saviour, in conscious imitation of the divine vision through which St Francis received his stigmata, the impression of the five wounds of Christ. The Elector's 'stigmata' was his imprisonment for the Confession of Augsburg.

8 Calvin and Geneva: the second generation of reform

The final major variant of evangelical reform to emerge during the first half of the sixteenth century is that associated with John Calvin and Geneva. Although usually included among the 'Swiss reformers', Calvin was by birth, education and temperament a Frenchman. In all his years at Geneva, he thought of himself as an exile and longed to extend his sphere of influence inside his native land. However, he died in 1564 without seeing the full implications of the 'reformed religion' (as it was known in the sixteenth century, rather than 'Calvinism'). Calvin belonged to the 'second generation' of reformers. He was born in Noyon in Picardy in 1509, a quarter of a century later than Luther or his contemporaries. He developed a different spirituality and different approach to reform that made him impatient with the compromises and half-way reforms characteristic of Lutheranism. He sought to purge the 'remnants of popery' from evangelical religion and to create a religion 'truly reformed' – hence the contemporary name adopted by his followers. As with Luther, the form of 'reformed religion' adopted or advocated by his followers was not always that which Calvin himself would have wished.

8.1 Calvin's conversion

Characteristic of Calvin's understanding of religion was the powerful sovereignty of God, reflected here in this autobiographical fragment describing his conversion experience.

It so happened that . . . I transferred to the study of law in obedience to my father's wishes. But God by his secret providence eventually steered me in a different direction. At first I was so obstinately devoted to the superstitions of the papacy that I was not easily extricated from such a mire . . . Then, by a sudden conversion, my heart was changed and shaped towards docility . . . I was immediately inflamed 5 with a desire for true piety and although I did not let my other studies lapse, I pursued them with less alacrity . . . God so moved and transformed me through a variety of twists and turns that I was allowed no peace until, contrary to my natural inclinations, he brought me to see the light.

Corpus Reformatorum, vol. 59, col. 22

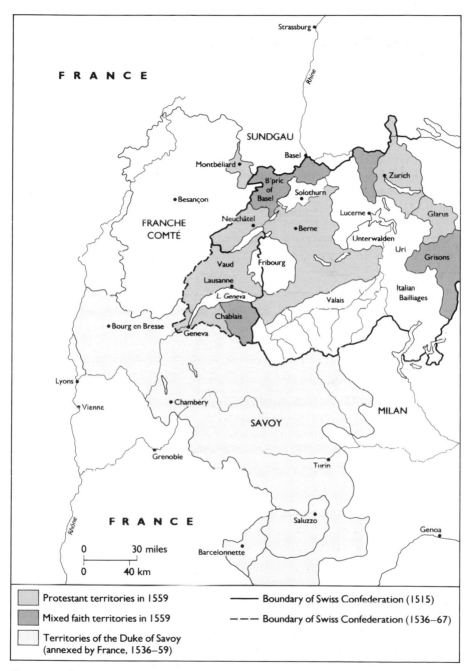

Geneva and its Neighbours in the Time of Calvin
(Based on map in G. R. Potter & M. Greengrass, *John Calvin* (Edward Arnold, 1983).)

8.2   Calvin's call to Geneva

In 1533 Calvin's evangelical convictions led him to flee from Paris into
exile in Basel. His indignation at the persecution visited on evangelical
believers in France moved him to write the first version of his *Institutes of
the Christian Religion* setting out the nature of his faith and in part justifying
his decision to flee. The publication of this work gained him an immediate
reputation in evangelical circles. After a short visit to France, he intended
to return to Basel and possibly Strassburg, but found himself almost by
accident in Geneva, and presented with a challenge.

8.2(a)   *From Theodore Beza's* Life of Calvin

Beza was Calvin's successor as leader of the church in Geneva. His
biography of Calvin provides the stock Calvinist account of the origins and
development of the 'reformed religion'.

After settling his affairs [in France] . . . he intended returning to Basel or
Strassburg, but all the roads were closed because of the war and he was forced to
travel through Switzerland. Thus he came to Geneva, without having thought of
this city, but brought thither by Providence, as afterwards appeared. A short time
before, the Gospel of Christ had been most wondrously introduced into that city   5
by the exertions of two illustrious men, namely Guillaume Farel from
Dauphine . . . and Pierre Viret of Orbe . . . In passing through Geneva Calvin paid
them a visit . . . Farel, a person obviously inspired with a kind of heroic spirit,
strongly urged him, instead of proceeding further, to stay and work with him there.
But in vain, until Farel addressed him thus: 'I declare in the name of the Lord, the   10
Lord will punish you for seeking your own interest rather than his.' Calvin,
terrified by this fearful denunciation, submitted to the wishes of the presbytery and
the magistrates, by whose suffrage, the people consenting, he was not only chosen
preacher (this he had at first refused), but was also appointed Professor of Sacred
Literature – the only office he was willing to accept. This occurred in August 1536.   15

Corpus Reformatorum, vol. 49, col. 125

8.2(b)   *Calvin's account*

I had taken care in my travels to conceal that I was the author of [the *Institutes*] and
I had resolved to continue dissembling, until at length Guillaume Farel detained
me in Geneva, not so much by counsel and exhortation, as by a fearful
imprecation, as if God from heaven had laid a violent hand upon me . . . A little
while before, popery had been driven out by the work of those illustrious men   5
Farel and Pierre Viret; but matters were not yet brought to a settled state and the
city was divided into vile and dangerous factions.

Corpus Reformatorum, vol. 59, cols. 23–4

Questions

1   How would you evaluate **8.1** and **8.2** as sources. Mention their strengths and weaknesses.
2   How far do you think Calvin's account of his conversion may have influenced his account of his call to Geneva.
3   How influential was Calvin, and how substantial was his reputation before he arrived in Geneva?
4   On what was that reputation based?

8.3   Calvin's first period in Geneva

The Reformation had been introduced in Geneva between March and May 1536, more or less as it had been elsewhere in Swiss or German towns, by first allowing preaching of the Word of God, then by prohibiting Catholic preaching and the celebration of the Mass, and finally by a vote of the governing council to accept the new belief. Thus Calvin arrived after the formal repudiation of papal belief and the acceptance of an evangelical reformation. Calvin's contribution was to draft a statement of reformed belief and to insist on a 'confession of faith' which all citizens and inhabitants of Geneva were to swear to uphold. Although the council soon accepted this 'confession', there was widespread opposition to it within the citizenry as a whole, bitterly dividing the city.

8.3(a)   *Formal acceptance of reform: minutes of the Council of 200, 21 May 1536*

Following the resolution of the council, a general assembly was summoned by bell and trumpet according to custom. The syndic Claude Savoye proposed that those who were opposed to the changes should speak out and explain why they did not wish to live according to the Scriptures and God's holy Word such as had been preached daily in the city since the abolition of Masses, and other papal abuses.   5
Since only one person spoke against it, it was generally agreed by a show of hands and a promise and oath taken before God that we would live in future according to his holy evangelical law and the Word of God, and that we should abandon all Masses, other ceremonies and papal abuses and everything relating to them. It was also unanimously agreed that someone of suitable knowledge should be employed   10
to teach in a school without charging any fees and that all parents should be required to send their children to school and make them learn there.

Corpus Reformatorum, vol. 49, cols. 201–2

8.3(b)   *Calvin's measures of reform*

Calvin then published a short formula of Christian doctrine, adapted to the church
of Geneva . . . To this he added a Catechism . . . briefly setting out the main points
of belief. Afterwards, along with Farel and Augustin Courault [an elderly, blind
monk who had previously preached in Paris before joining Farel in Geneva],
Calvin's first objective was to obtain, at a meeting attended by the whole city, an   5
oath forcing the entire population to abjure the papacy and adhere to the Christian
religion and its discipline, as comprehended under a few headings. Most of
Calvin's colleagues kept aloof from this struggle through timidity and some of
them, to his great unease, even secretly impeded the work of the Lord. As was to
be expected in a city which had just been delivered from the snares of the duke of   10
Savoy and the yoke of Antichrist, and in which factions still greatly prevailed, some
citizens refused to take the oath but by the good hand of the Lord, on 20 July 1537
(the clerk of the city taking a leading part), the council and people of Geneva
solemnly declared their adherence to the leading doctrines and discipline of the
Christian religion.   15

Corpus Reformatorum, vol. 49, col. 126

8.3(c)   *Opposition to the confessional oath*

Register of the Council of 24
    12 November 1537. It was reported that yesterday the people who had not yet
made their oath to the reformation were asked to do so, street by street; whilst
many came, many others did not do so. No one came from the German quarter. It
was decided that they should be commanded to leave the city if they did not wish to
swear to the reformation.   5
    26 November 1537. Some people have been reported to have said that it was
perjury to swear to a confession which had been dictated to them in writing . . .
[Farel or Calvin] replied that if the contents of the written confession were studied
carefully it would be seen that this was not so, but that it was a confession made
according to God. Examples from holy Scripture (in Nehemia and Jeremiah)   10
proved that the people should all be assembled to swear to keep faith with God and
observe his commandments.

Register of the Council of 200
    2 January 1538. It was reported that certain slanders against the preachers were
being spread around the town. It was decided that the matter should be passed on
to the lieutenant for investigation and prosecution.
    16 January 1538. It was said that many people in the city and its suburbs
repeated slogans which divided the city, and that these originated with some
drunkards who went about the town at night from one tavern to another saying
'You are brothers in Christ' and other similar phrases mocking the preachers. It
was decided that an investigation should be conducted into this.

Corpus Reformatorum, vol. 49, cols. 216–17, 219–20

8.4 Discipline in Calvin's scheme of reform

A great part of the conflict provoked by Calvin in Geneva revolved around his belief that discipline was necessary to enforce and consolidate reform. In Calvin's view, this may have been a necessary means of promoting upright Christian life, but it may have been perceived by the Genevans, who had just rejected 'papal tyranny', as a new form of oppression. In January 1537, Calvin and Farel submitted to the town council a proposal for the establishment of a form of discipline in Geneva, the basis of what later became the consistory.

Our lord established excommunication as a means of correction and discipline, by which those who lead a disorderly life unworthy of a Christian and who refuse to mend their ways and return to the right path after they have been admonished, are expelled from the body of the church and cut off as rotten members until they come to their senses and acknowledge their fault . . . So if there is in us any fear of 5 God, this ordinance should be enforced in our church.

To accomplish this we have determined to beg you to establish and choose, according to your good pleasure, certain persons of virtuous life and repute among all the faithful, constant and not easy to corrupt who shall be assigned and distributed in all quarters of town to keep an eye on the life and conduct of every 10 individual. If one of these sees any obvious vice which should be reprehended, it shall be brought to the attention of one of the ministers, who will admonish the person at fault and fraternally admonish them to amendment. If it is plain that such remonstrances are to no avail, the person shall be warned that such obstinacy will be reported to the church. 15

Should it appear that the sinner proposes to persevere in his or her hardness of heart, it will be time to excommunicate. The offender will be regarded as cast out from the companionship of Christians and left in the power of the devil, until good proof has been given of penitence and amendment. In sign of this casting out, the sinner shall be excluded from communion and the faithful forbidden to converse 20 with him or her.

Corpus Reformatorum, vol. 38, cols. 9–10

Questions

1 Why was Calvin not satisfied with the kind of reformation introduced before he came to Geneva? Why did he believe more rigorous reform was necessary? What forms of discipline did he propose?

2 Why did some Genevans respond so negatively to Calvin's proposals? Why might some of Calvin's fellow preachers have been less than enthusiastic for his ideas on reform? (See 8.3(b).)

3 Consider the reliability and bias of the sources in 8.3 and 8.4.

4   How far do you think Calvin was responsible for the 'factions' [**8.3(b)**,
     line 11] he sees as plaguing Geneva?
5   What other conflicts might have been in play in these questions of
     religious reform? (What is the significance of the opposition from the
     'German quarter' mentioned in **8.3(c)** [**line 3**]?)
6   Consider the respective roles of the ministers or preachers and the
     magistrates in effecting reform. How active was the population at large
     in its introduction?

8.5   Calvin and Farel leave Geneva

The growing conflict in Geneva turned around the respective authority of
the ministers and the secular magistrates. However, there was also ethnic
conflict involved: the German merchant community, who leaned towards
the German-speaking Protestants of Berne, were suspicious of the growing
influence of French émigrés led by Calvin. In February 1538 the annual
town council elections turned against Calvin's faction, with four syndics
elected who were hostile to the French preachers and determined that the
magistrates alone should decide religious policy. The breach came when
the canton of Berne produced a form of communion service intended to
create uniformity among the various evangelical churches in its territory.
The Genevan council insisted on adopting the Bernese form of communion, which Calvin and Farel in their turn refused to accept. They were,
therefore, dismissed. However, subsequent Calvinist historiography represented the issue in a rather different light.

8.5(a)   *From the minutes of the town council, 19 April 1538*

A letter was received from Berne concerning the observance of communion . . .
enquiring whether we also wished to observe the ceremony as contained therein. It
has been decided by the Great Council to do so. If there are no objections, it is
proposed that the said letter be shown to the ministers Farel and Calvin, and that
they should be asked if they want to observe the said ceremonies or not . . .   5

It was resolved that communion [on Easter Day, 21 April 1538] should be
observed, if possible, according to the form of the said letter from Berne. The
ministers Calvin and Farel are to be asked if they will preach accordingly . . . M. de
Soultier then returned from Calvin and Farel and reported that they did not want
to preach or celebrate communion according to the said letter.   10

Corpus Reformatorum, vol. 49, cols. 223–4

8.5(b)　*Theodore Beza's version of events*

The Gospel had, as we have said, been admitted into the city and popery been
abjured. At the same time there were many who had not renounced the flagrant
immoralities which had so long prevailed in a city subject for so many years to
monks and a corrupt clergy; and many old feuds, which had originated during the
war of [independence from] Savoy between some of the first families still　　　　5
subsisted. An attempt was made to remove these feuds, first by gentle admonition,
and later by severe rebuke, but to no avail. The evil increased so much that the city
was split into parties by the factious doings of a few individuals, not a few of whom
positively refused to conform to the order they had sworn to observe. Matters
came to such a pass that Farel and Calvin, men endowed with a noble and heroic　　10
spirit . . . declared they would not dispense the Lord's Supper to people so much
at odds among themselves and so estranged from all ecclesiastical discipline.

Corpus Reformatorum, vol. 49, col. 127

8.6　Calvin's return to Geneva, September 1541

Calvin spent the period after his dismissal from Geneva in Strassburg. It
was another swing in the political pendulum that enabled his return, when
his faction was successful in the elections in 1540. After initial reluctance,
he was reinstated as preacher, at the request of the Small and Great
Council, a fact that greatly increased his authority. He immediately set
about introducing the ecclesiastical ordinances that were to give effect to
his vision of a truly reformed community. This did not remove factional
conflict in Geneva, but intensified it.

8.6(a)　*Minutes of the council, 13 September 1541*

Master John Calvin, Minister of the Gospel. The same has arrived from
Strassburg and presented himself to the council . . . Afterwards he made some
apologies at length for his delayed arrival. That done, he stated that it was
necessary to set about the work of ecclesiastical ordinances. Resolved, that they
would apply themselves to it immediately.　　　　　　　　　　　　　　　　　5

Corpus Reformatorum, vol. 49, col. 282

8.6(b)　*Beza outlines the consequences*

As soon as he returned to the city . . . the first thing he did was to obtain the
consent of the town council to a form of ecclesiastical polity which was agreeable to
the Word of God, and from which neither ministers nor people should afterwards
be permitted to depart. That which had formerly been approved was hated by
some of the common people and also by some of the leading citizens who, though　5
they had renounced the pope, had assumed the name of Christ in name only.

Some of the ministers who had also remained in the city when these good men
[Calvin and Farel] were driven out – the chief of whom was afterwards accused of
flagrant misconduct and basely deserted his post – did not dare to resist the
testimony of their consciences, but secretly opposed it and would not easily allow   10
themselves to be brought to order. They were also not lacking in excuses for their
malice, by pointing to churches in which there was no excommunication. Indeed,
there were those who cried out that a popish tyranny was being re-established. But
Calvin overcame these difficulties through firmness and singular moderation. He
demonstrated that it was not only doctrine but also the form of church government   15
that must be sought in Scripture . . . He was thus successful in securing those laws
of ecclesiastical polity, which the church still observes, to be drawn up with
universal consent, read out and finally approved by the suffrage of the people on
20 November 1541.

Corpus Reformatorum, vol. 49, col. 133

Questions

1 What was at stake in Geneva in Calvin's expulsion from and recall to
  Geneva? What were the main objections of those who continued to
  oppose him?
2 How far did Calvin's victory depend on politics?
3 Contrast Beza's account of these developments with the evidence
  offered by the town council minutes.

8.7 The Ecclesiastical Ordinances

Calvin differed from Luther and Zwingli in holding that the form of church
government was firmly specified in Scripture, and that a church could not
therefore be truly reformed unless its structure accorded with this form.
The Ecclesiastical Ordinances of 1541 both embodied this form of
government and laid down guidelines on how it should work.

First, there are four orders of offices instituted by our Lord for the government of
his church: namely, pastors, doctors, elders and deacons.

Pastors
Pastors are sometimes named in the Bible as overseers, elders and ministers.
Their work is to proclaim the Word of God, to teach, admonish, exhort and
reprove publicly and privately, to administer the sacraments and to apply fraternal   5
correction, along with the elders or their deputies.

The selection of pastors
First, the ministers should choose someone suitable for the office. Then he is to be
presented to the council. If he is thought suitable, he will be accepted and received

by the council. He is then given a testimonial to be produced when he preaches to
the people, so that he can be received by the common consent of the assembly of   10
the faithful. If he is found to be unsuitable and this is shown by legitimate proof,
there must be a new selection to find another . . . After election he must take an
oath of allegiance to the government following a written formula.

In order to maintain purity and harmony in their teaching, all the ministers
should meet together once a week to hold discussions about the Scriptures. No   15
one shall be excused unless there is good reason for absence.

If any differences of opinion concerning doctrine should arise, the ministers
should gather together and discuss the matter. If necessary they should call in
elders commissioned by the government to assist in the settlement of any
disagreement. Finally, if they cannot reach agreement, due to the obstinacy of one   20
of the parties concerned, the matter shall be placed before the magistrates for final
decision.

Teachers

The proper duty of teachers is to instruct the faithful in sound doctrine so that the
purity of the Gospel is not corrupted by ignorance or evil opinions . . . The order
nearest to the ministry and most closely associated with the government of the   25
church is that of lecturer in theology who gives instruction on the Old and New
Testament. But since no one can profit from such teaching without first being
instructed in languages and in the humanities, . . . it will be necessary to establish a
school to teach the young, to prepare them not only for the ministry but for civil
government . . . These teachers shall be under the same ecclesiastical discipline as   30
the ministers. There shall be no other school in the city for small children; the girls
shall have a separate school as hitherto . . . No one shall be appointed unless he is
first presented by the minister to the council for approval.

Elders

Their office is to keep watch over the lives of everyone, to admonish amiably those
they see in error and leading disorderly lives. Wherever necessary, they shall make   35
a report concerning these persons to the ministers, who will be designated to
make fraternal correction . . . As our church is now arranged, it would be most
suitable to have two elected from the members of the Small Council, four from the
Council of Sixty and six from the Council of 200 . . . They should be chosen from
each quarter of the city so as to be able to maintain supervision over all. They are   40
to be chosen as follows. The Small Council will be asked to nominate the most
suitable men they can discover. In order to do this, they should discuss the matter
with the ministers and then present their suggestions to the Council of 200 for
approval. If they are found worthy, they must take an oath in the same form as that
presented to the ministers.   45

Deacons

There were two orders of deacons in the ancient church, the one deputed to
receive, distribute and protect the goods of the poor . . . the other to take care of

the sick and administer the pittance for the poor . . . The election of the deacons is
to be conducted as that of the elders . . . It will be the deacons' task to take diligent
care that the hospital is well administered and that it is open not only to the sick   50
but also to aged persons who are unable to work, to widows, orphans and other
impoverished persons. Those who are sick are to be kept in a separate lodging.

Corpus Reformatorum, vol. 38, cols. 14–24 *passim*

Questions

1   How do Calvin's ideas on doctrine and church organisation differ from
    those of Luther and Zwingli?
2   Calvin claimed to model his church structure on that of the early
    church. What evidence can you find for this in Geneva?
3   What was the role of the secular magistrates in Calvin's church
    structure?
4   It has sometimes been said that Calvin instituted a 'theocracy' in
    Geneva. What is meant by a 'theocracy'? Does **8.7** support this claim?

8.8   Calvin on civil government

Unlike Luther, Calvin attributed a most positive role to civil government in
the work of reform, although he saw its chief work as the positive
promotion of godliness. Calvin was certainly no democrat in any modern
sense, believing that tyranny could be preferable to anarchy (as he would
have called modern democracy!), although he believed that aristrocratic
rule was the best form of all. Nor was Calvin in favour of rebellion or
resistance to authority: resistance even to an ungodly ruler was permissible
only to certain persons and under strictly defined circumstances.

8.8(a)   *Calvin on the authority of civil government (1536)*

Civil government has as its appointed end to cherish and protect the outward
worship of God, to defend the sound doctrine of piety and the position of the
church, to adjust our lives to civil society, to shape our social behaviour to civil
righteousness, to reconcile us with one another and to promote general peace and
tranquillity. All this I admit would be superfluous if the Kingdom of God as it now   5
exists within us were to put an end to temporal life.

All agree that no state can be happily constituted unless its first care is to
promote piety; and that laws which, ignoring the law of God, concern themselves
with men only are absurd. Since religion therefore holds pride of place for all the
philosophers, and since this has always been supported by the universal consent of   10
all nations, Christian princes and magistrates should be ashamed of their insolence
if they neglect this duty . . . All this demonstrates the folly of those who wish

magistrates to concentrate solely on doing justice among men to the exclusion of matters of religion, as though God would create offices in his name to settle temporal disputes, but would omit a matter of vastly greater moment, namely the   15 pure worship of himself according to the order of his law.

Institutes of the Christian Religion, edited by J. T. McNeill, London, 1960, pp. 1487, 1495

8.8(b)   *Calvin on the best form of government*

If you compare the forms of government [monarchy, aristocracy, democracy] among themselves apart from their circumstances, it is not easy to distinguish which one of them excels in usefulness, for they contend on such equal terms. The fall from monarchy to tyranny is easy; but it is not much more difficult to fall from the rule of the best men to the faction of a few; yet it is easiest of all to fall 5 from popular rule to sedition. If the three forms of government which the philosophers discuss are considered in themselves, I will not deny that aristocracy, or a system compounded of aristocracy and democracy, far excels the others; not indeed in itself, but because it is very rare for kings so to control themselves that their will never disagrees with what is just and right; or for them to have been   10 endowed with such acuity and prudence to know how much is enough. Therefore man's weakness causes it to be safer for a number of men to exercise government so that they can help one another teach and admonish the others. If one of them asserts himself unfairly, there are a number of censors and masters to restrain his wilfulness.   15

Institutes, p. 1493

8.8(c)   *Obedience to magistrates*

Let no one be deceived here. The magistrate cannot be resisted without God being resisted at the same time . . . Moreover under this obedience I include the restraint which private citizens ought to bid themselves to keep in public, so that they do not deliberately intrude in public affairs, or needlessly interfere in the office of a magistrate, or undertake anything at all political. If anything in a public 5 ordinance requires amendment, they should not raise a tumult or try to correct it themselves, but should commend the matter to the judgement of the magistrates . . . We are not only subject to the authority of princes who perform their tasks towards us uprightly and faithfully as they ought, but also to the authority of all those who, by whatever means, have control of affairs, even though   10 they perform only a minimum of the prince's office.

Institutes, pp. 1511–12

8.8(d)   *When and how resistance is possible*

We must in the meantime be very careful not to despise or violate that authority of
magistrates, full of venerable majesty, which God has established by the weightiest
decrees, even though it may reside with the most unworthy men, who defile it as
much as they can through their own wickedness. For if the correction of unbridled
despotism is the Lord's to avenge, let us not at once think that he has entrusted it   5
to us, to whom no command has been given except to obey and suffer.

I am speaking here of private individuals. If there are any magistrates appointed
by the people to moderate the power of kings (as in ancient times the ephors were
set up against the Spartan kings, or the tribunes of the people against the Roman
consuls, or the demarchs amongst the senate of the Athenians; and perhaps as   10
things now are, such power as the three estates exercise in every realm where they
hold their chief assemblies) I am so far from forbidding them to withstand, in
accordance with their duty, the fierce licentiousness of kings, that, if they wink at
kings who violently fall upon and assault the lowly common folk, then I declare
their dissimulation involves nefarious perfidy, because they dishonestly betray the   15
freedom of the people, of which they know they have been appointed protectors by
God's ordinance.

Institutes, pp. 1518–19

8.9   Calvin on the role of a godly ruler

To the Duchess of Ferrara, 8 January 1564
I beg you to keep a firm hand, to the utmost of your power, to establish a good
discipline for repressing vice and scandals. I do not mean regulation with regard to
political matters, but also in respect of the consistory of the church, and let those
who are established to keep an eye on the conduct of others be godfearing men of   5
holy life and of such sincerity and straightforwardness that nothing shall prevent
them from doing their duty, having such a zeal as becomes them in maintaining the
honour of God in its integrity. Now let no one, whatever his rank or condition . . .
be ashamed to submit to the order which the Son of God has himself established,
and bend his neck to receive the yoke. For I assure you, Madame, that without this   10
remedy there will be an unbridled licentiousness which can only engender
confusion. Those who make some profession of Christianity will be for the most
part dissolute. In short, there will be a pliant and as it were, many-coloured
Gospel, for we see how everyone flatters himself and is disposed to follow his own
appetites.   15

Thus, Madame, to have a church truly reformed it is more than ever requisite to
have people charged with a superintendence to watch over the morals of each; and
that no one may feel aggrieved in giving an account of his life to the elders, let the
elders themselves be selected by the church, as nothing can be more reasonable
than to preserve to it this liberty, and this privilege will tend also to produce greater   20
discretion in the choice of fitting men, and approved of as such by the
consistory . . . It is right that you should be reminded of one thing, namely that at

all times the devil has striven by sinister reports and defamation to render the
ministers of the Gospel contemptible in order that they may become the object
either of aversion or disgust. For that reason the faithful should be carefully on   25
their guard against such wiles . . . If there are any who aim even indirectly to
discourage you from pursuing what you have so well begun, you ought to shun
them like a deadly plague. And indeed the devil stirs them up by indirect means to
alienate people from God, whose will is that he should be recognised in the person
of his servants.   30

Corpus Reformatorum, vol. 48, cols. 231–3

Questions

1. What did Calvin envisage as the tasks of secular government?
2. What did he believe the best form of government to be?
3. Compare Calvin's views on obedience to those of Lutheran authorities.
4. Under what circumstances was resistance to unjust government justified?
5. Who could and who could not resist unjust rule?

8.10   The workings of the consistory

The consistory in Geneva was a unique organisation, and it became the main means of enforcing and ensuring the continuation of piety in Calvin's vision of a 'church truly reformed'. Its power depended on its ability to excommunicate and on its close relationship with the secular magistrates. Although it was formally constituted of laymen, the pastors also sat on it, and as the Company of Pastors increased in size, they came to have a strong voice in its affairs. For contemporaries, the Genevan consistory was the hallmark of the reformed religion, and Calvin held no church to be truly reformed where the consistory was not established. However, its thoroughness quickly earned it the label of a 'new popish tyranny', and there was strong opposition to it from the outset, as well as to Calvin as the dominant figure behind it.

8.10(a)   *The statutory provisions*

If anyone shall wilfully contradict received doctrine, he shall be summoned to
appear. If he recants, he shall be dismissed without prejudice. If he is stubborn, he
shall be admonished from time to time until it shall be evident that he deserves
greater severity. Then he shall be excommunicated and this action be reported to
the magistrate.   5
    If anyone is negligent in attending worship to such an extent that a noticeable
contempt is evident for the communion of the faithful, or if anyone shows himself

contemptuous of ecclesiastical discipline, he shall be admonished . . . [as above, etc.]

For the corrections of personal faults . . . secret vices shall be dealt with secretly 10 and no one shall be brought before the church for accusation if the fault is neither notorious nor scandalous, unless he has been found to be recalcitrant.

As for obvious and public evil, which the church cannot overlook, if the faults only merit admonition, the duty of the consistory shall be to summon those concerned, to remonstrate with them amicably in order that they may be reformed, 15 and if they mend their ways, to let the matter rest. If they persevere in evil doing, they shall be admonished again [etc. as above].

Nevertheless, all these measures shall be applied in moderation. There shall not be such a degree of rigour that anyone will be oppressed, for all corrections are intended to be medicinal, to bring sinners back to the Lord.   20

Corpus Reformatorum, vol. 38, cols. 29–30

8.10(b)   *Cases before the consistory*

30 March 1542: Jane Petreman was questioned about her faith because she had not received the Sacrament and has attended Mass. Professed her faith and believes in one God, wants to come to God and the holy church, and has no other faith. Said the Lord's Prayer in Latin, and said that she believes as the church believes . . . Questioned as to why she does not content herself with the Sacrament 5 as celebrated in this town but goes elsewhere: replied that she goes where it [the Sacrament] seems good . . . Has been excommunicated again, has to appear from day to day, and has not wanted to renounce the Mass.

25 May 1542: Aymon Peronet was summoned because of certain medicines and cures for the sick, and for using certain spells which are forbidden by God, which 10 words he uses in the course of his business; asked if he would like to live according to the reformation. About the refusal of rent, he replied that his father had required no licences, nor used any spells; and that he made plasters from wax, cobbler's wax and scalding steam and mixed them all together. Sometimes he resided in Lyon . . . and sometimes in this town, and uses only everyday words, 15 such as 'In the name of the Father and of the Son'. He says that he wants to live according to the Lord and lords of his country, and that he lived according to the place where he found himself. Asked if he went to sermons, he replied 'Yes', and that he had not taken the Sacrament because he had not been here very long.

17 June 1546: Gaspard Favre, to whom remonstrances had been made . . . 20 because he had been found celebrating a service in a garden near St Gervais; when questioned whether an assembly of Christians had been there, he had replied 'Yes'. Remonstrances had been made to him, warning that he should not be allowed to leave the congregation of the faithful, for which attempt he was banned from the Sacrament. Said that he did not think that he had offended God by that. 25 Asked if he recognised the rebellion he committed by saying he would not reply to M. Calvin, which spoke for itself: he replied that he had said he would put his reply in writing; for remonstrances had been made to him, Favre, in strongly rebellious words, and M. Calvin had said to him 'We here are above you.' He had

replied that he knew very well indeed that M. Calvin was above all. Following such 30
rebelliousness, M. Calvin left the consistory. Resolved: that the lords of the
Council be told that the entire consistory would resign until Favre received such
punishment as he deserves.

Corpus Reformatorum, vol. 49, cols. 293, 296, 382–3

8.11 Calvin's opponents and critics in Geneva

Both Calvin's austere view of reformed piety as well as the thoroughness of
the consistory aroused much opposition. Sometimes it seemed as though
the consistory existed merely to suppress criticism of Calvin and his fellow
ministers. The consistory's right to excommunicate was also seen as crucial
by supporters and critics. Once this right had been firmly established, it
was able to crush most opposition. Some of the strongest dissent was
directed against Calvin personally and the issue Calvin chose on which to
attack his critics, that of having a too carefree lifestyle – wearing
fashionable clothes, dancing or feasting. This was a lifestyle favoured by an
elite group around Ami Perrin, a member of one of Geneva's wealthiest
and most distinguished families, and from 1547 captain-general of the city
militia. Led by Perrin, members of the family constituted some of Calvin's
most severe critics, and the Perrin faction found a certain sympathy among
the youthful militia, whose exuberance was seen as a focus for misrule in
the city. Calvin accused Perrin and his associates of moral depravity,
labelled them as 'libertines' and repeatedly used this charge to attack his
opponents.

8.11(a) *Attempts to limit the consistory*

19 March 1543: Council of Sixty. It has been raised here whether the consistory
has the power to prohibit the blameworthy from receiving the Sacrament of the
Lord, whereupon it was resolved that the consistory has no jurisdiction or power of
prohibition, but only that to admonish and must refer delinquents to the council,
so that their lordships may consider judgement on them according to their 5
unworthiness.

Calvin to Viret, 24 March 1543: we have recently had a dispute with the council,
but it was settled immediately. The syndic announced to us in the consistory that
the council had reserved the right of excommunication to itself. I immediately
stipulated that this decree would be confirmed either with my death or exile. The 10
following day I called together the Company of Pastors; on their advice I
demanded from the syndics that there be an extraordinary meeting of the council.
They reluctantly agreed. I made a long and grave speech there about the matter
and gained what I sought without any dispute.

Corpus Reformatorum, vol. 49, col. 309; vol. 39, col. 521

8.11(b) *Pierre Ameaux and his wife*

Registers of the council, 27 January 1546: It was disclosed that Pierre Ameaux had
said that M. Calvin was a wicked man, was no more than a Picard and preached
false doctrine . . . Ordered that he be taken prisoner and a charge be drawn up
later.

Calvin to Farel, 13 February 1546: More than fifteen days have already passed   5
here since the cardmaker [Ameaux] has been held in prison because he abused me
with such great vehemence at a dinner in his house that it was clear that he was out
of his mind. I bore it impassively, except that I testified to the judges that it would
not displease me if they dealt with him with the severity of the law. I wished to visit
him, but access was forbidden me by decree of the council. However, certain good   10
men accuse me of cruelty because I avenge my injuries so pertinaciously.

Registers of the council, 8 April 1546: Having seen the reports, from which we
perceive that he [Ameaux] has spoken wickedly against God, the magistrates and
the minister M. Calvin . . . Ordered, that he be condemned to do a circuit of the
town in his shirt, bareheaded and carrying a lighted taper in his hand; he is then to   15
come before the tribunal on his knees, crying for mercy to God and justice,
confessing that he has spoken evilly; he is also condemned to pay all expenses, and
the sentence is to be publicly announced.

Corpus Reformatorum, vol. 49, cols. 368, 377; vol. 40, col. 284

8.11(c) *Calvin and the 'libertines'*

Calvin to Viret and Farel, 20 April 1546: After your departure the dancing
provided more business for us than I had thought. All who were there were called
before the consistory, with the two exceptions of Corne [Syndic and president of
the consistory!] and Perrin [the captain-general], and they impudently lied to God
and to us. I became enraged as the indignity of the matter was presented, and   5
abused them severely for their contempt of God, because sacred adjurations had
been introduced for nothing and . . . they persisted in their contumacy . . .
Francisca Perrin [sister of Gaspard Favre] is even more of a railer than Favre was a
pest to us . . . I asked what home would be sacrosanct, what law would be free, for
we were already holding the father [of this family] on a conviction for adultery; the   10
trial of another was at hand; there was a great rumour about a third: the brother
had openly derided and condemned us and the council. I added that a new city
should be built for them in which they could live apart . . . but as long as they
remain in Geneva, I would have laboured in vain unless they obeyed the laws.
Meanwhile the husband has retired to Lyon, hoping that the matter would be   15
quietly buried there. By taking an oath they would be forced to confess the truth.
Corne warned that they would by no means be allowed to perjure themselves.
They confessed not only what we wished, but also that on the same day they had
danced with the widow of Balthasar Sept. All were thrown into prison: the Syndic
was a worthy example of moderation . . . However, he was admonished more   20
severely in the consistory and deposed from his position until he gave testimony of
repentance.

Registers of the council, 24 June 1547: The ministers and the consistory are greatly aggrieved at the wife of Amy Perrin, remonstrating with her because she danced and insulted the minister M. Abel, calling him 'filth' and many other   25
sinister words; it was necessary that she be brought to order. Ordered that she surrender herself to prison, and that Jean Blanquet be put in charge of the prison while she is held prisoner there, since the warder of the prison is a servant of the house of Perrin.

Corpus Reformatorum, vol. 40, cols. 334–5; vol. 49, col. 407

8.11(d) *Jacques Gruet's attack on Genevan government, July 1547*

Do not rule yourselves by the word or will of one man. For you see that men have many and diverse opinions amongst them! Each in turn wishes to be governed in his own fashion . . . and frequently the opinion of one man alone will cause much misfortune . . . If there is one person who is of melancholic temperament and hates everything contrary to his melancholy, he desires, if he has the power, that   5
everyone be melancholy like himself. And if he has this pre-eminence and authority, he will want his nature to be set in execution . . . Why does it seem to me that the council, in order to quench all contrariety, makes one estate such that no one may object to the subjection of a people for something contrary to nature . . . ? But I am a man who, wanting to eat, will do so according to what pleases me . . . If   10
I want to dance, leap, lead a joyful life, what business is that of justice? None. For each time this crudest form of justice engenders many machinations, one man is able to be the cause of several evils and the perdition of a thousand men.

Sentence on Gruet: We the Syndics and judges of criminal causes in this city of Geneva, having seen the case . . . against you, Jacques Gruet, and your voluntary   15
confession, in which we see that you have greatly offended and blasphemed God, contravening his sacred Word, and you have also perpetrated things against the magistrates, menaced and spoken evilly of the servants of God, and committed the crime of lese-majesty, and so have merited corporal punishment. We condemn you . . . to have your head chopped from your shoulders, your body tied to the   20
gallows and the head buried, so that you should end your days as an example to others who might wish to commit this crime.

Corpus Reformatorum, vol. 40, cols. 564–5, 567

Questions

1 What was at stake in the conflicts over the consistory?
2 Was the consistory acting oppressively?
3 Compare Calvin's version of the opposition to him with the other accounts provided in **8.10** and **8.11**, especially those of his opponents. Discuss in class who was more justified in their behaviour, Calvin or his opponents.
4 How far were these conflicts over politics as much as religion?
5 Reconsider the question about theocracy in the light of **8.10** and **8.11**.

8.12   Doctrinal deviation in Geneva

Geneva was also plagued with doctrinal disputes, although none of those who challenged Genevan orthodoxy seems to have had any considerable following. Some more outspoken dissidents appear to have been punished merely in the name of a strict orthodoxy, which had the effect of making Genevan belief look narrow and intolerant. Two cases aroused wider interest, that of Jérôme Bolsec, a doctor of theology, physician and former Carmelite monk who had enthusiastically embraced Calvin's notion of reform. The second was the Spanish scholar and theologian Michael Servetus, whose fertile, confused and often obscure ideas led him to advocate universal toleration and to disbelief in the Trinity. Bolsec was accused of deviant doctrines on freewill and predestination, while Servetus was charged with antitrinitarian belief. Bolsec was exiled from Geneva, but Servetus was burned. More than any other episode, Servetus' death at the stake occasioned the charge that Geneva represented a narrow intolerance worse than the papacy.

8.12(a)   *Jérôme Bolsec*

Registers of the Company of Pastors, 16 October 1551: . . . M. Jérôme Bolsec continued presenting his false propositions about election and reprobation, denying that they were 'from eternity' and saying with great protests and exhortations that one must recognise any other election or reprobation than that which one sees in believing or not believing; and that those who consider God to   5
have an eternal will by which he has ordained some to life and some to death are making a tyrant of him as the peasants made an idol of Jupiter . . . saying that this would be heresy, and that such doctrine would involve great scandal, since one would have to believe that St Augustine was of this opinion, which can be shown to   10
be an error. Further, one would have distorted several passages of Scripture in order to support this false and perverse doctrine . . . adding several other calumnies and blasphemies through which he showed well the venom that he had hidden in his heart, watching for an opportune time to spew it out in public.

On the spot, M. Calvin replied to him by reaffirming this doctrine, which had been for so long faithfully taught in the church with the common consent of all   15
those edified by it since the beginning of the Gospel; and point by point replied to him about all his slanders, so that the assembly was satisfied and greatly edified by the doctrine he deduced from passages [of Scripture] concerning election and reprobation. When the congregation of pastors was finished, one of the assistants of the lieutenant, who was present there, . . . seeing the scandal which the said   20
Jérôme had committed in the church and the blasphemies he had uttered against God and his doctrine . . . took him prisoner . . . and his trial was commenced as was customary with such people.

Corpus Reformatorum, vol. 36, col. 146

8.12(b)   *Michael Servetus*

(i) The doctrine of the Holy Spirit as a third separate being lands us in practical tritheism no better than atheism, even though the unity of God be insisted upon. Careful interpretation of the usual proof texts shows that they teach not a union of three beings in one, but a harmony between them. The Holy Spirit as a third person of the Godhead is unknown in Scripture. It is not a separate being, but an   5 activity of God himself. The doctrine of the Trinity can neither be established by logic nor proved from Scripture, and is, in fact, inconceivable.

Two Treatises of Servetus on the Trinity, Cambridge, Mass. 1932, p. 3

(ii) Calvin to Farel, 26 October 1553: There was unanimous agreement that the impious errors of Servetus with which Satan formerly disturbed the church, now monstrously repeated, were not to be tolerated. Those of Basel agreed; those from Zurich were most vehement of all in their approval. The gravity of his wickedness was accepted by them and they urged our council to deal with him severely. Those   5 of Schaffhausen agreed . . . The stage Caesar, who for three days had pretended to be ill, finally faced the court to receive the penalty for his crimes. He had the nerve to ask that the matter should come before the Council of 200. He was however unanimously condemned. Tomorrow he is to be brought to execution. We have tried in vain to alter the manner of his death. Why we were unsuccessful,   10 I may be able to tell you later.

Corpus Reformatorum, vol. 42, col. 657

8.13   Calvin's final victory in Geneva, 1552

Registers of the council, 9 November 1552: Extraordinary meeting of the council . . . on the *Institutes of the Christian Religion* of M. Calvin. All considered, the council decided and concluded as follows: all things having been well understood, it is announced and decreed that the said book is well and sacredly made, and its doctrine is God's holy doctrine . . . and henceforth no one is to speak   5 against the said book nor against the doctrine therein; it is ordered that other parties and all persons [in Geneva] should observe this decree.

Corpus Reformatorum, vol. 49, col. 525

Questions

1   What evidence do you find in **8.12** to support the view that the Genevan faith was narrow and harsh?

2   List the various opponents of Calvin described in **8.10–8.12**. Using columns, state the reasons for their opposition and the means by which they were punished. Assess Calvin's role in their punishment.

3   How do Calvin's religious principles as you have encountered them in this chapter explain his treatment of doctrinal opposition?

4   How would you explain Calvin's ultimate success in dominating Geneva?

Themes for comparative investigation

The following questions should be pursued by reading comparatively through several documents or chapters, following the development of broader themes. They are especially suitable for class projects.

1 Construct a chart setting out the points of agreement and main points of difference among the reformers mentioned in the documents.
2 Make a list of the reformers found throughout the documents and assess their respective contribution to the Reformation. State clearly the criteria you have used for assessing 'contribution'.
3 Consider the different attitudes to reform of (a) the clergy compared with laypeople;   (b) the clergy compared with secular magistrates; (c) laypeople compared with magistrates;   (d) townsfolk compared with countryfolk.
4 Using the illustrations throughout the book, discuss the importance of visual media for the communication of Reformation ideas. Make a list of the different kinds of ideas presented by the images alone. How did accompanying printed text amplify or change the visual message?
5 Discuss the main stages the campaign for religious reform passed through in the years 1520–64. What possibilities for reform came to nothing? Why did reform take the direction it did by mid-century?
6 Study the maps provided and locate the places or territories in which the various documents were produced or to which they were sent. What can you deduce about geographical patterns in the Reformation?
7 How did secular, and especially political interests influence the nature of religious reform. Were they a help or a hindrance?
8 Compare the nature and progress of reform in the countryside with that in the towns.
9 Why did religious reform seem to change so little in popular religion?
10 Consider the significance of the devil in the reformers' understanding of the religious revival of the Reformation.
11 Consider the role of millennialism in the progress of the Reformation.
12 How would you assess the 'success' or 'failure' of the Reformation?

Suggestions for further reading

Some of the books listed below give general background for the period, some are concerned primarily with religious matters, others with political issues. Luther has exercised a stronger magnetic pull on historians than the other reformers, but it should be possible to gain some understanding of many more of them. The most fruitful approach is to relate the individual personalities to their contemporaries and notice the reactions of different groups in town and countryside, both positive and negative.

General surveys

John Bossy, *Christianity in the West 1400–1700*, Oxford University Press, 1985
Euan Cameron, *The European Reformation*, Oxford University Press, 1991
A. G. Dickens, *The Age of Humanism and Reformation*, Prentice Hall, 1972
G. R. Elton, *Reformation Europe*, Fontana, 1967
M. Hughes, *Early Modern Germany 1477–1806*, Macmillan, 1992
Alister McGrath, *Reformation Thought. An Introduction*, Oxford University Press, 1988
New Cambridge Modern History, vol. 1, Cambridge University Press, 1961
New Cambridge Modern History, vol. 2, 2nd edn, Cambridge University Press, 1990, chs 3–7
S. E. Ozment, *The Age of Reform 1250–1550*, Yale University Press, 1980
B. M. G. Reardon, *Religious Thought in the Reformation*, Longman, 1981
L. W. Spitz, *The Protestant Reformation 1517–1559*, Harper & Row, 1985

The Reformation in Germany and Switzerland

Peter Blickle, *The Revolution of 1525*, Johns Hopkins University Press, 1981
Peter Blickle, *The Communal Reformation*, Humanities Press, 1992
William Bouwsma, *John Calvin. A Sixteenth-century Portrait*, Oxford University Press, 1988
Thomas A. Brady, *Turning Swiss, Cities and Empire 1450–1550*, Cambridge University Press, 1985
A. G. Dickens, *The German Nation and Martin Luther*, Collins/Fontana, 1976
Hans-Jürgen Goertz, *The Anabaptists*, Routledge, 1994

Harro Höpfl, *The Christian Polity of John Calvin*, Cambridge University Press, 1982

R. Po-Chia Hsia (ed.), *The German People and the Reformation*, Cornell University Press, 1988

R. Po-Chia Hsia, *Social Discipline and the Reformation*, Routledge, 1989

K. Leach, *The German Reformation*, Macmillan, 1990

Bernhard Lohse, *Martin Luther. An Introduction to his Life and Work*, T. & T. Clark, 1987

Alister McGrath, *A Life of John Calvin*, Blackwell, 1990

Michael Mullett, *Luther* (Lancaster Pamphlets), Methuen, 1986

H. A. Oberman, *Luther. A Man between God and the Devil*, Yale University Press, 1989

S. E. Ozment, *The Reformation in the Cities*, Yale University Press, 1975

T. H. L. Parker, *John Calvin. A Biography*, Dent, 1975

G. R. Potter, *Zwingli*, Cambridge University Press, 1976

Keith Randell, *Luther and the German Reformation*, Arnold, 1988

Keith Randell, *Calvin and the Later Reformation*, Arnold, 1988

Tom Scott, *Thomas Müntzer*, Macmillan, 1989

R. W. Scribner, *The German Reformation*, Macmillan, 1986

R. W. Scribner, *Popular Culture and Popular Movements in Reformation Germany*, Hambledon Press, 1986

R. W. Scribner, *For the Sake of Simple Folk. Popular Propaganda for the German Reformation*, Oxford University Press, 1993

W. P. Stephens, *The Theology of Huldrych Zwingli*, Oxford University Press, 1988

W. P. Stephens, *Zwingli. An Introduction to His Thought*, Oxford University Press, 1992

James D. Tracy (ed.), *Luther and the Modern State in Germany*, Sixteenth Century Journal Publishers, 1986

G. H. Williams, *The Radical Reformation*, Weidenfeld & Nicolson, 1962 (revised edition, Sixteenth Century Journal Publishers, 1993)

Collections of documents

John Dillenberger (ed.), *Martin Luther. Selections from his Writings*, Doubleday, 1961

Hans J. Hillerbrand (ed.) *The Reformation in its Own Words*, SCM Press, 1964

Hans J. Hillerbrand (ed.), *The Protestant Reformation*, Harper & Row, 1968

S. M. Jackson (ed.), *Ulrich Zwingli 1484–1531. Selected Works*, University of Pennsylvania Press, 1972

G. R. Potter, *Huldrych Zwingli*, Arnold, 1978

G. R. Potter and M. Greengrass, *John Calvin*, Arnold, 1978

E. G. Rupp and Benjamin Drewery, *Martin Luther*, Arnold, 1970

G. Strauss, *Manifestations of Discontent in Germany on the Eve of the Reformation*, Indiana University Press, 1971

Glossary

abjuration   formal renunciation, involving an oath

antinomianism   belief that Christians who are saved are not bound to observe a strict moral code

asceticism   severe self-discipline practised as a religious observance

Catechism   simple form of religious teaching set out in booklet form and using question and answer method

chiliasm   belief that the end of the world is fast approaching, cf. **millennialism**

consecration   blessing, especially of bread and wine in the Eucharist

consistory   pre-Reformation church court, adapted by Protestants for discipline of morals and manners; it became the most important disciplinary organ of Calvinism in Geneva and elsewhere

diet   political assembly similar to a modern parliament

dispensation   exemption from religious rule or observance

Elevation   lifting up of bread and wine for adoration of the congregation after consecration in the Mass

Eucharist   Catholic name for the communion, involving bread and wine consecrated during the Mass

evangelical reform   religious reform based on the principles of the Gospel and Word of God, initially inspired by Luther's religious ideas

iconoclasm   breaking or destruction of religious images or statues in belief that they are idolatrous

iconography   systematic description of visual contents of an image; so the pattern of images making up the theme in a depiction

liturgy/liturgical   relating to the form and conduct of church services

millennialism   belief in the coming of the rule of the saints before the imminent end of the world

ordinance   law, decree, edict

predestination   belief that God has, from the beginning of time, destined some to eternal life, others to damnation; particularly associated with Calvin, who formulated the doctrine more elaborately than other reformers

presbytery   ruling body of pastors

purgatory   state of existence between heaven and hell, where those with only minor sins are purged before entering heaven

sacramentals   blessed objects for pious use by Christians (salt, palms, candles, herbs), popularly believed to have protective powers against the devil and other form of harm

sacramentarian   one who denied the real presence of Christ in the Eucharist and asserted a mere symbolic presence

schism   split within the church

Septuagint   Greek version of the Old Testament

theocracy   form of government in which the state is ruled by the laws of God; therefore one in which the clergy play a dominant role in government

visitation   inspection of church, either parish by parish or of individual parishes; pre-Reformation conducted by the bishop, in Reformation carried out by the state with the aid of clerical and secular bureaucrats

Index